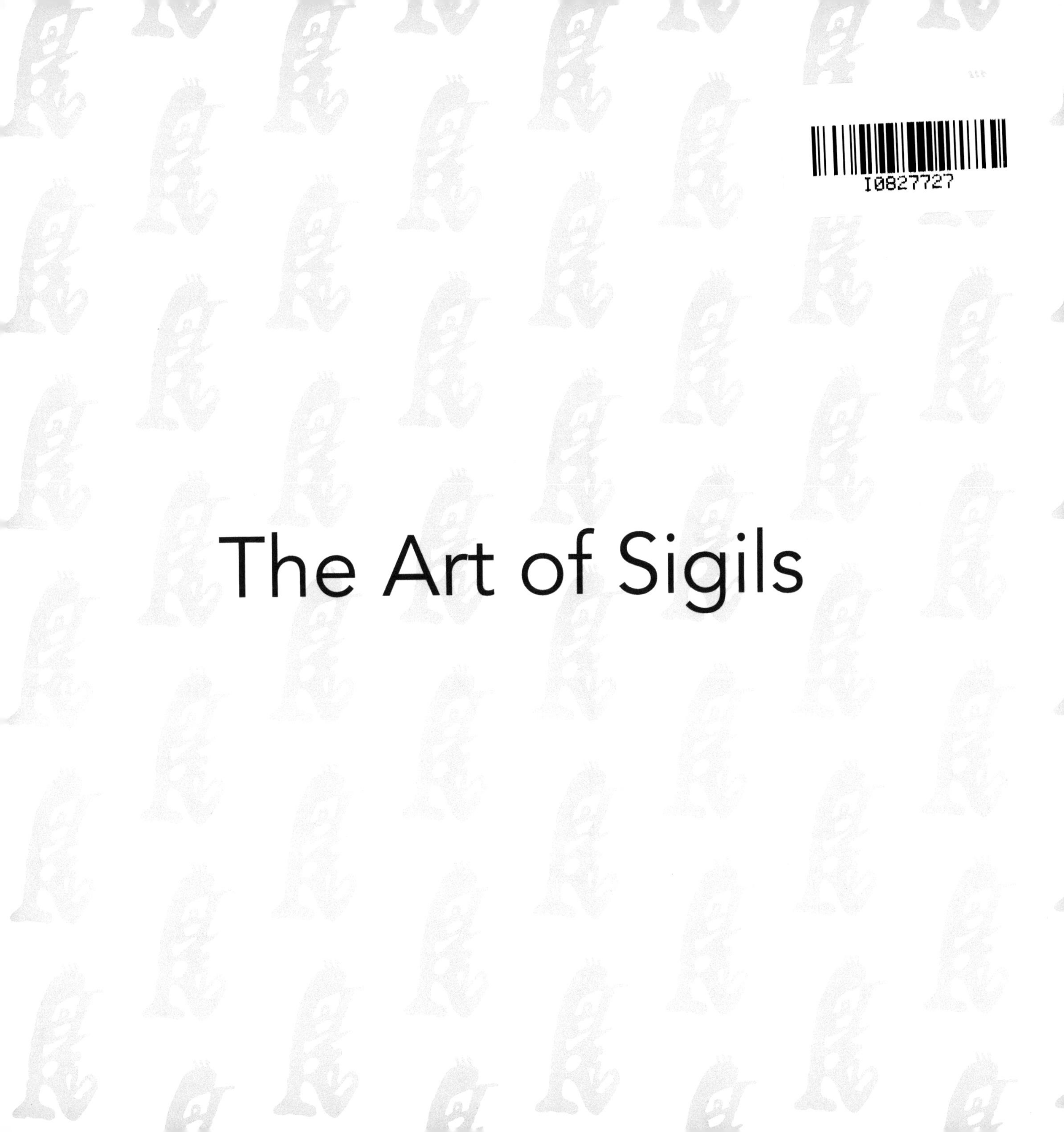

The Art of Sigils

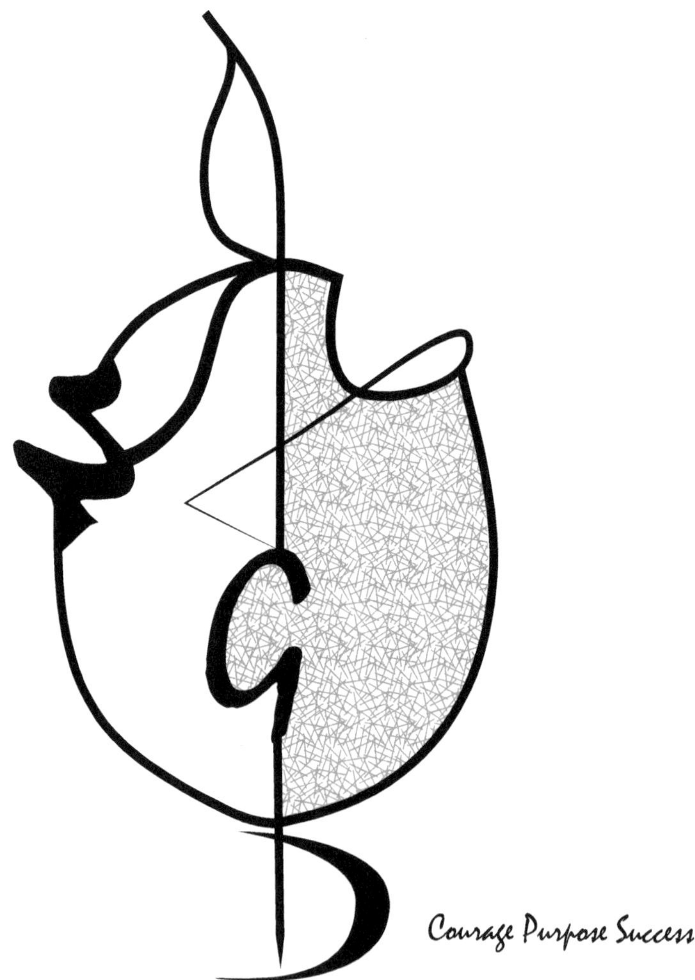
Courage Purpose Success

The Art of Sigils
by Gina Leslie

Library of Congress Control Number: 2018943759

TheArtOfSigils.com

Cover design by Gina Leslie
Title treatment by Mandy Gough

ISBN 978-1-7322045-0-08

Dedication

This book is dedicated to the idea that we ALL are creative in some way.

I hope this sparks your imagination and helps you tap into your own dormant creativity.

Give yourself permission to explore, have fun, make mistakes, learn stuff!

Table of Contents
& List of Sigils

Acknowledgments

Thank you to my amazing friends for their talent, support and encouragement: Mandy Gough created a graceful and mysterious graphic motion piece, designed the title treatment for the cover and edited this book; Dr. Alfred Surenyan composed a beautiful piece of sigil inspired music; Kyrian Corona is my cheerleader and publicist; Ren Zatopec helped with my artist bio; Patti Negri helped me with the Indiegogo campaign video; my niece, Ana, helped me with photo shoots and many friends shared my posts and announcements on social media. A big thanks also to the people who had the courage to enter the Inspiring Creativity Contest: Lisa Vig, Amanda Jones, James Babwe, Chelsea Turner, Ian Chambers and Melody Hesaraky and to those who backed this project through the Indiegogo campaign: Alfred, Cora, Becky H, Brandy, Becky A, Alyson and Karen. Your support of this project is greatly appreciated!

The Art Of Sigils Summary

The dictionary defines a sigil as
"An inscribed or painted symbol considered to have magical power"

Sigils are commonly used in ceremonies or rituals to achieve a purpose or as the personal symbol of a wealthy and powerful person. King Solomon is said to have used sigils to compel daemons to build his temple. Kings and Popes often used sigils (in the form of rings) to seal personal messages and documents to ensure private transmission. But this book is not a history of sigils. Feel free to do your own investigation in that direction, if you wish. Libraries and the Internet will provide you with abundant information. Search The Key of Solomon, Kabalah, Austin Osmon Spare or simply the word sigils.

The Art of Sigils book is about looking beyond the magickal implications of sigils to discover that gateway to your own creativity. Getting started is often the hardest part. By starting with a sigil you are making a springboard to jump into a new creative endeavor. If you're feeling stuck it can even be a tool for getting past that creative block and back into the flow.

Discover Your Own Creativity
Using Ancient Magical Symbols

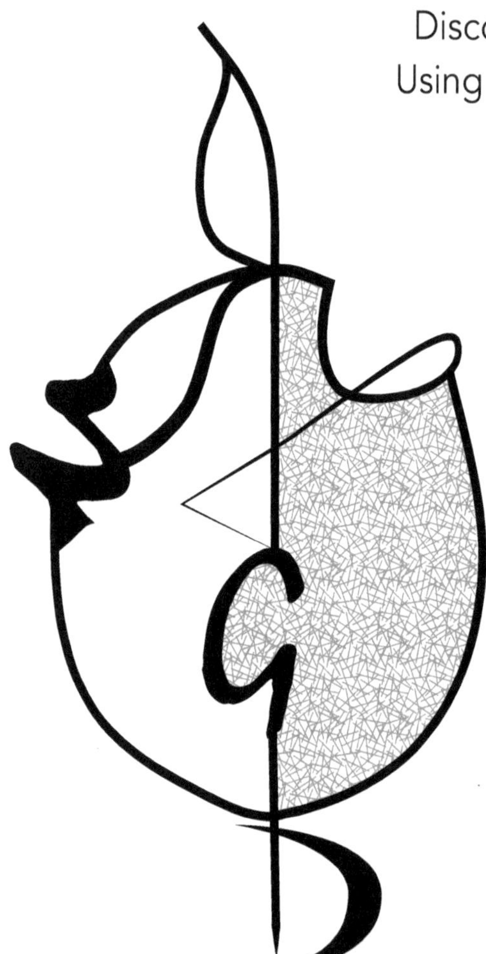

The Art of Sigils

by Gina Leslie

Sigils have been around since humans first started making marks on cave walls. Those of us who use sigils often think of them only in terms of magick and spells, or stamps in sealing wax. But have you considered that they have a wider potential as tools for creativity and can even be artwork in and of themselves? I have been making sigils for nearly 20 years and recently the sigils I'm making are evolving from simple sketches to full-fledged creative pieces, solely for the sake of art and creativity.

First let me point out that there is a difference between being Creative and being An Artist. While not everyone is an artist, I truly believe that most people are creative in some form. But, unless it can be monetized, our society so actively devalues art and creativity, or doesn't see the creativity underlying everything we come into contact with, that many people stifle their creative selves around the same time they put away their toys striving to be seen and accepted as "grown up". I see sigil making as a gateway for those who say, "I'm not creative", to actively tap into their own dormant, but inherent creativity. For an artist, or even life in general it can also be an effective visualization tool to move past or through whatever might be blocking your creative process.

If you do any amount of research on sigils, as I have, you will find all manner of complex and intimidating equations and formulas for sigil creation. An example of this is King Solomon's seal. You can see that it's quite a complicated design.

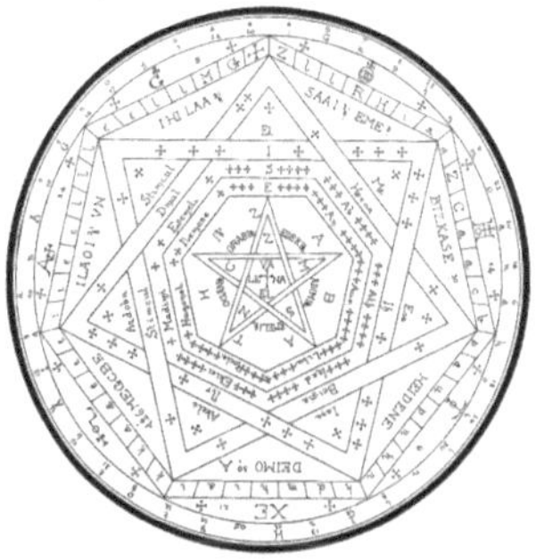

My process is neither complex nor intimidating; I write out words that have meaning to me and explore the shape and arrangement of the letters until I come up with a design that "feels" right to me. My technique is somewhat based on the ideas of Austin Osman Spare, a 19th century English artist and occultist, who used letter-forms to create his "alphabet of desire" and other magickal tools.

All of my images presented in this book started out as hand or computer drawn sketches that became "finished" pieces of art, in that I reached a point of satisfaction with the overall design and decided to stop. Creative people can "enhance" their creations until the cows come home. The trick is knowing when to stop and walk away.

I even give you a peek inside the thought process behind some of my pieces. Plus I gave friends and strangers two different Sigil Challenges to come up with their own creative works. I share their results with this method as examples of where you can go. I hope you enjoy them and that they inspire you to explore your creative side!

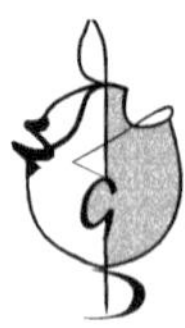

This is the one that started it all.

When I turned 50 I wanted to do something fun, something different to mark the occasion. So I decided to get a tattoo.

I didn't want just ANY tattoo out of a flash book. The design had to mean something to me. I think it took me three months to come up with a design that was simple and very personal.

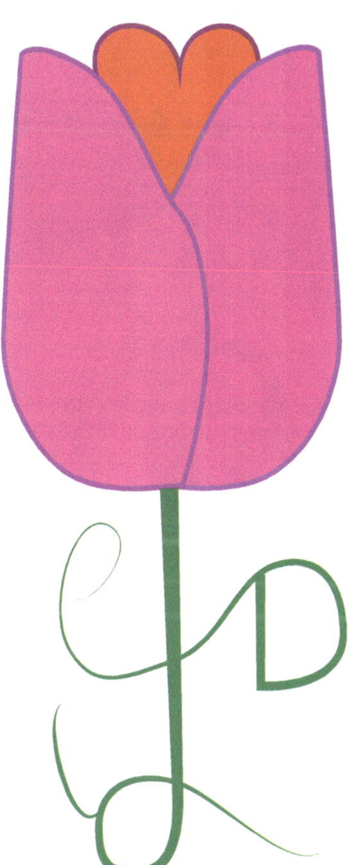

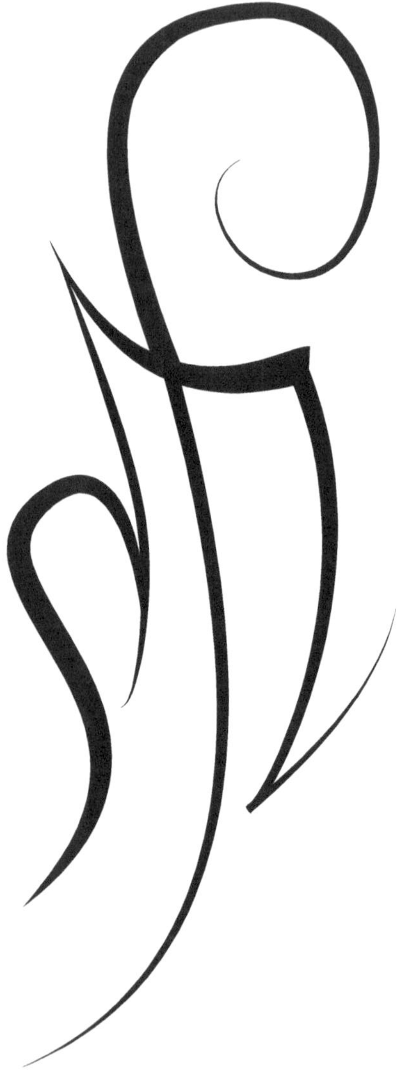

This sigil also became a tattoo. I liked the flow and delicate lines of this design.

Wanting to make sure I liked the look, I had it applied in henna to "test drive" it for a while before making the commitment.

This one reminds me to ...

Follow My Bliss

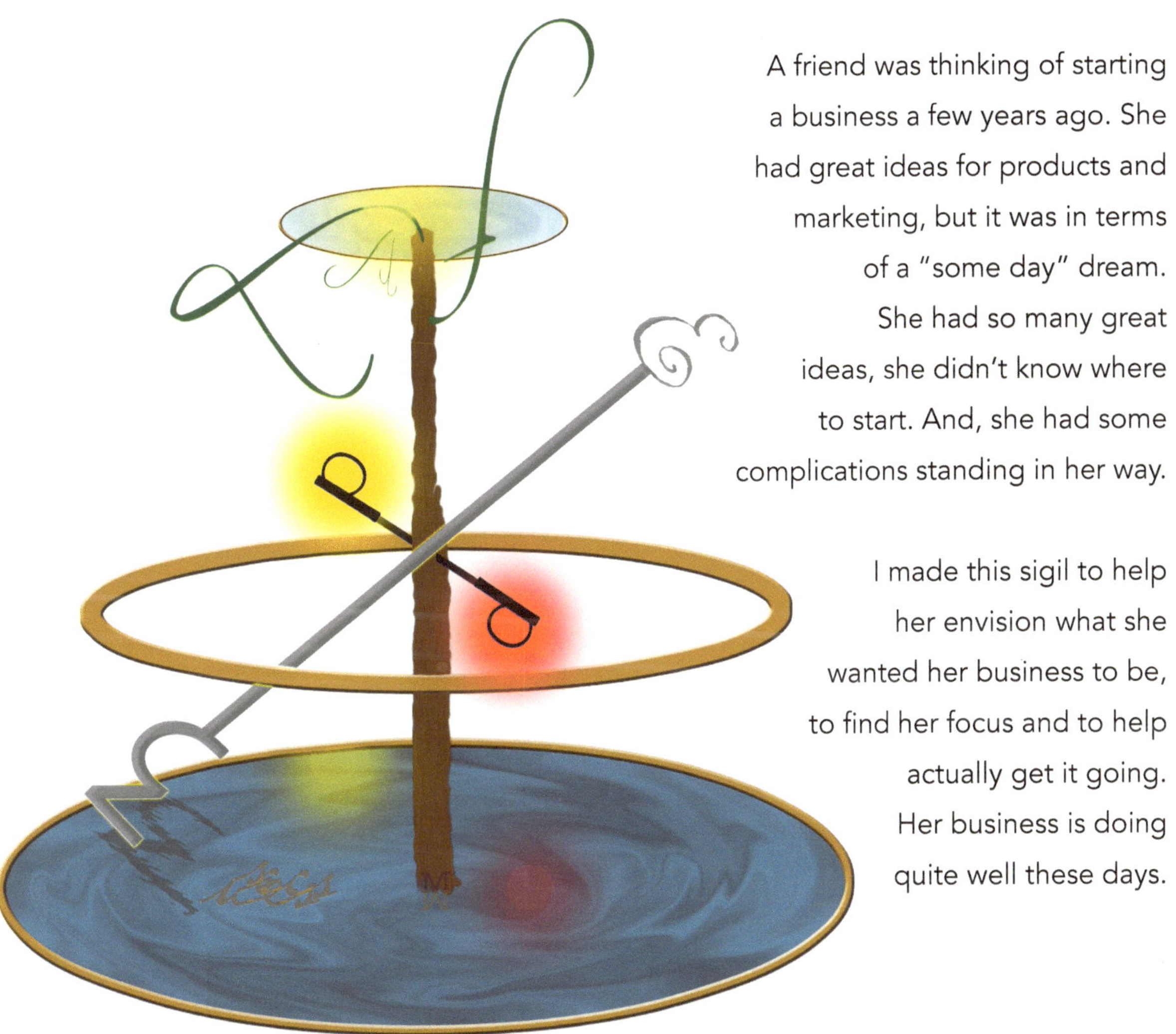

A friend was thinking of starting a business a few years ago. She had great ideas for products and marketing, but it was in terms of a "some day" dream. She had so many great ideas, she didn't know where to start. And, she had some complications standing in her way.

I made this sigil to help her envision what she wanted her business to be, to find her focus and to help actually get it going. Her business is doing quite well these days.

Balance Blend Integration Nexus

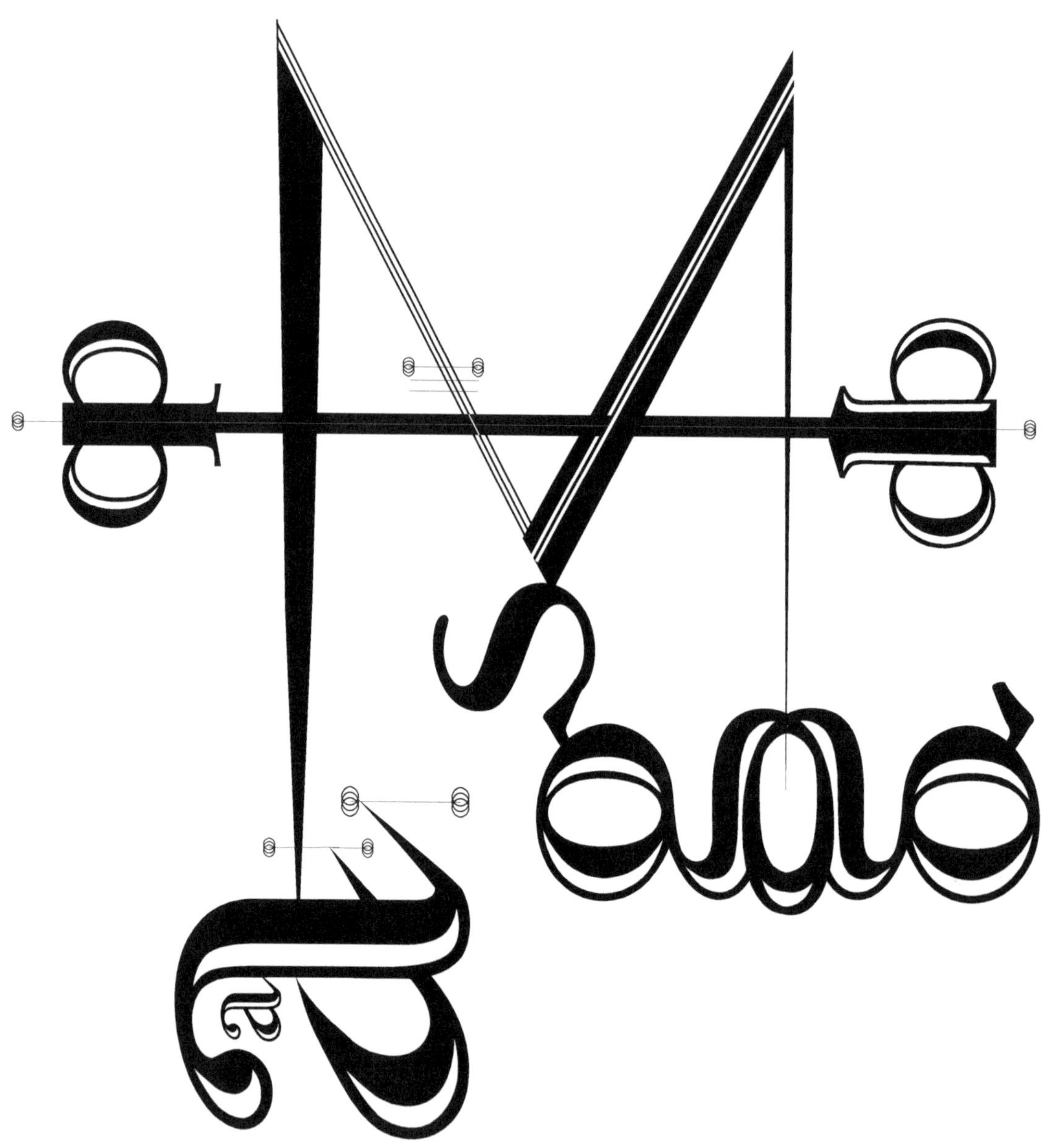

Wisdom Strength Compassion

I like the openness and clean lines of this image. Many times the letters become unrecognizable and sometimes they are the structure of the design (as in the image on the previous page).

Scanning the original sketches and bringing them into a design program allows me to try out different fonts and shape combinations. If you don't have a design program but want to play with drawing different font shapes, just look up fonts on-line or look through art and design books at your local library for inspiration.

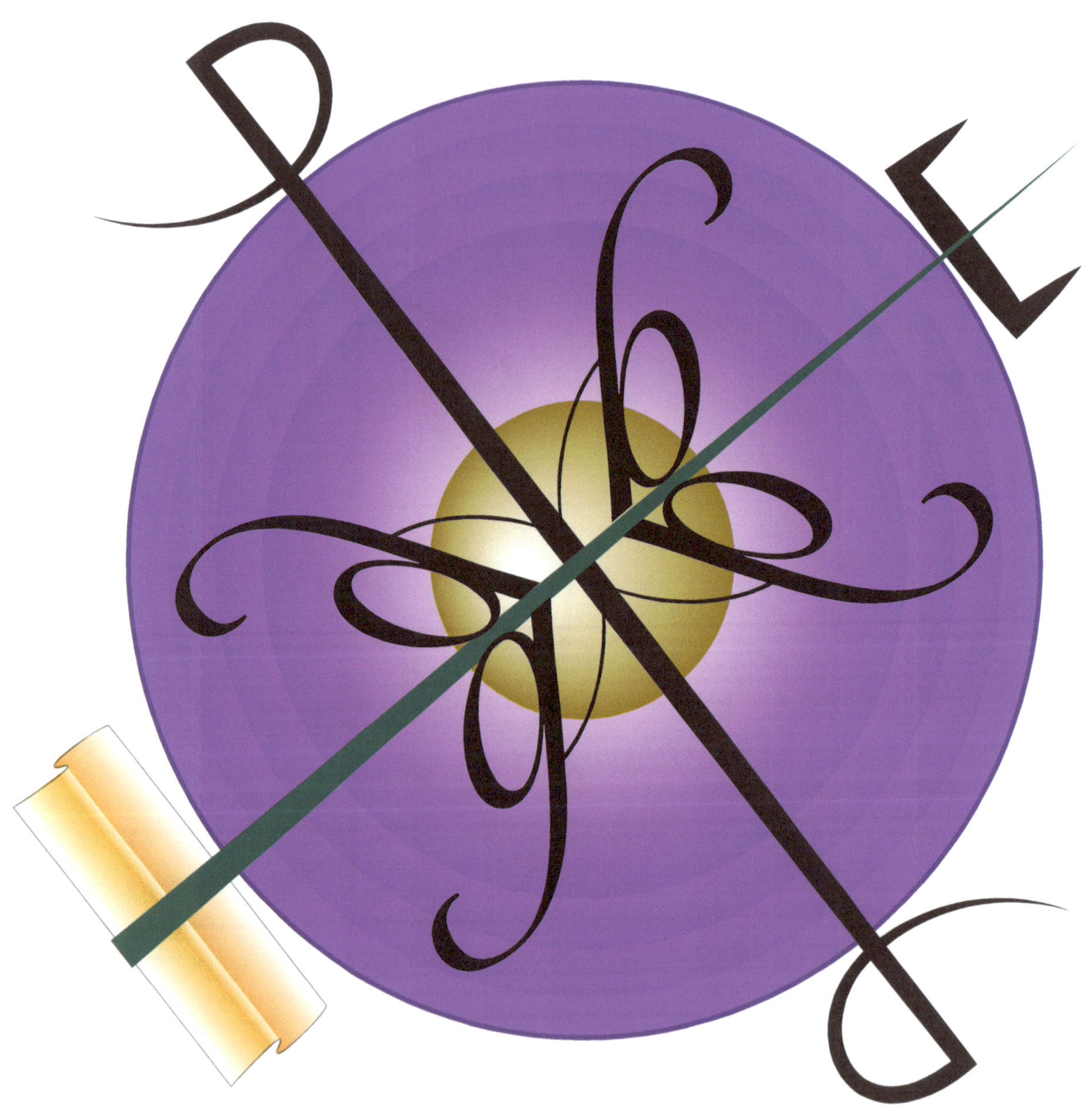

Inspire Success Profit

In creating a demonstration piece for a sigil making class, I wanted to show that the design could go beyond the sigil as a magickal tool, that it could become a piece of art in and of itself. This piece was the actual inspiration for the creative endeavor of writing The Art of Sigils.

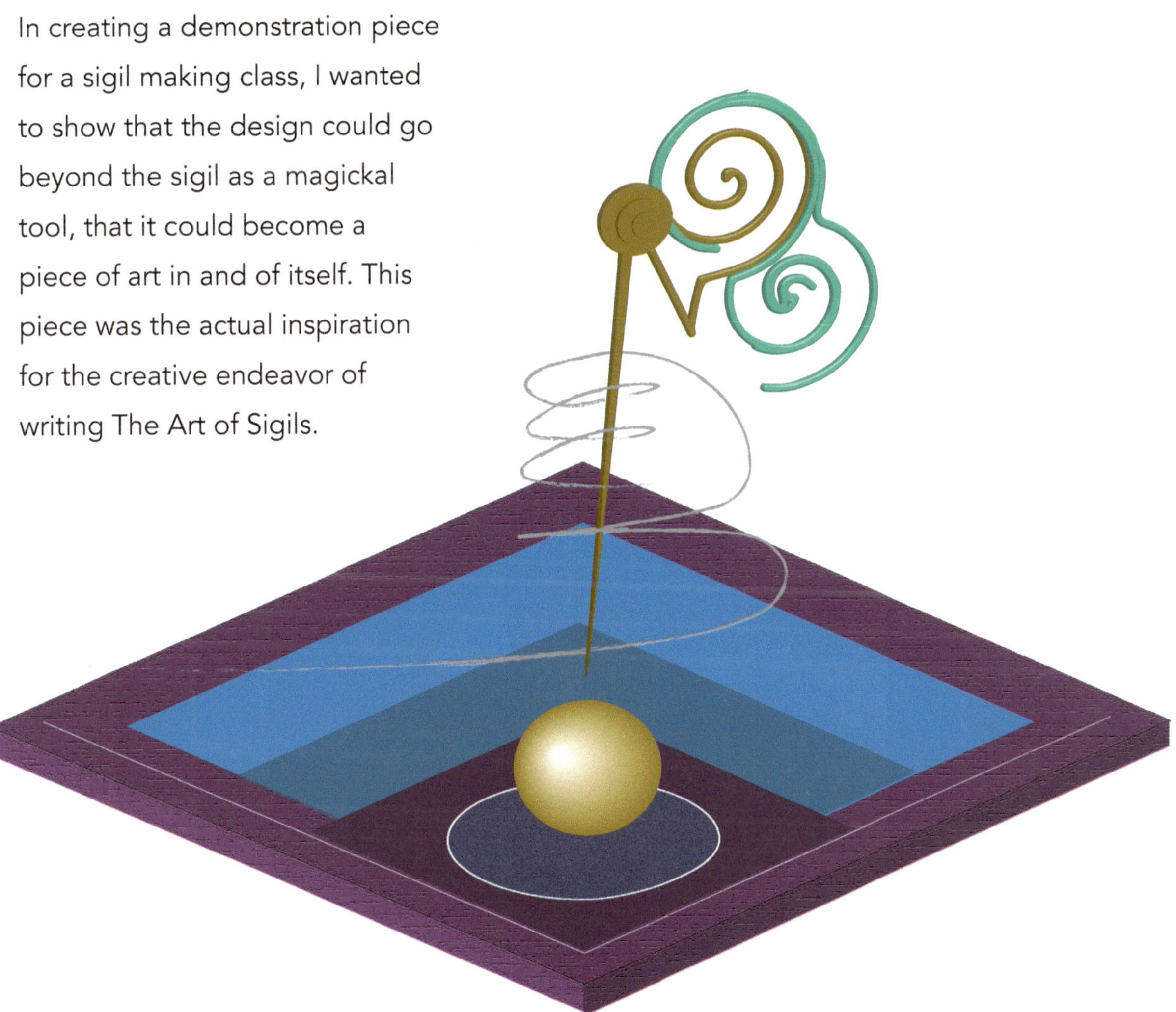

New Better Job

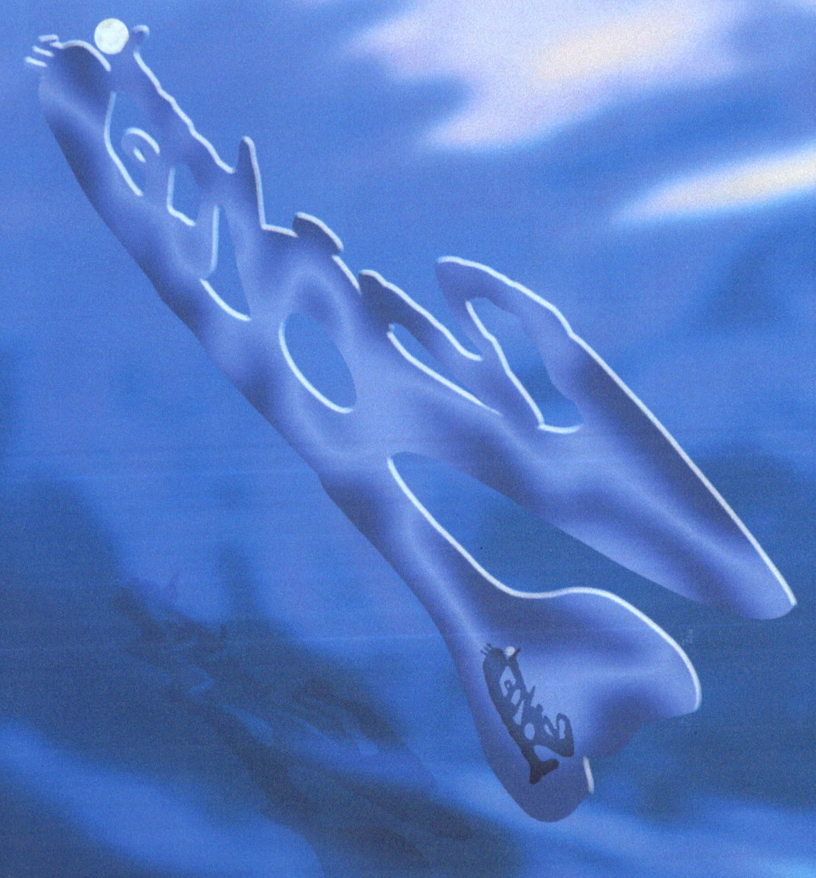

Pick Me

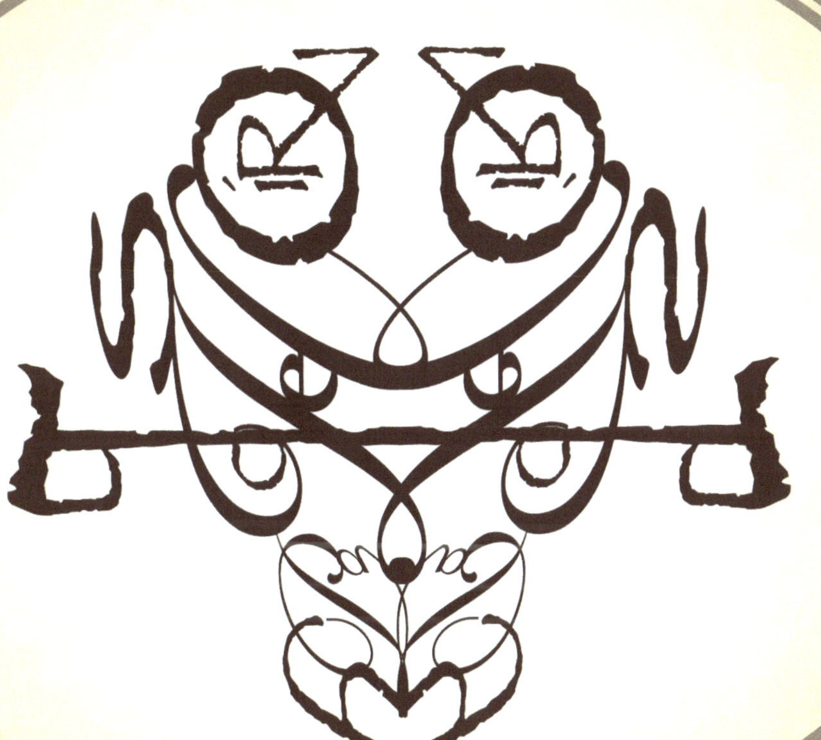

Prosperity Creativity Happiness

I work in a lot of arts and crafts disciplines - crochet, knitting, weaving, sewing, painting, photography, lampworking, jewelry, ceramics - just to name a few. Often my focus is on learning how to make things. I have an insatiable curiosity to learn how things are made and try it for myself. I get great satisfaction in making things by hand rather than buying a commercially available item. Because most of these endeavors require that I buy the raw materials, I look for ways to finance my crafty habit!

The following two sigils were both based on the same thought - Prosperity Through Creativity.

I made this piece as a title page graphic for a sigil making class I teach called "Manifesting Your Desires Using Sigils". As I was preparing this book, I had to go back to the original pencil drawing to make sure the title was correct. After all, there is no "g" or "b" in the original words, and I couldn't remember how they got into the design.

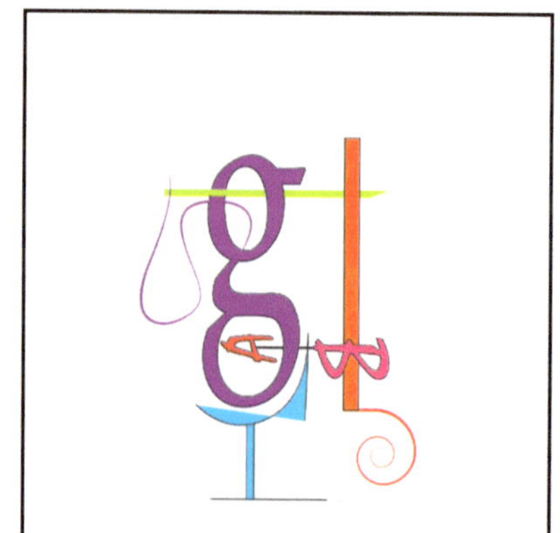

Then I remembered! The "g" is for my name, Gina. I wanted to make it very personal. The "b" just happened somehow. I suspect that it originally was a "p". I've learned to go with the flow where design quirks occur, considering them to be happy detours.

Did I mentioned sewing in that list above? The element that looks like a needle and thread is a nod to the custom capes that I make. The rod with the spiral underneath represents lampworking, which is another craft I have learned and intend to explore more deeply.

The next version of the Prosperity Through Creativity sigil started digitally. I took letters and pushed them around until I came up with a design I found interesting.

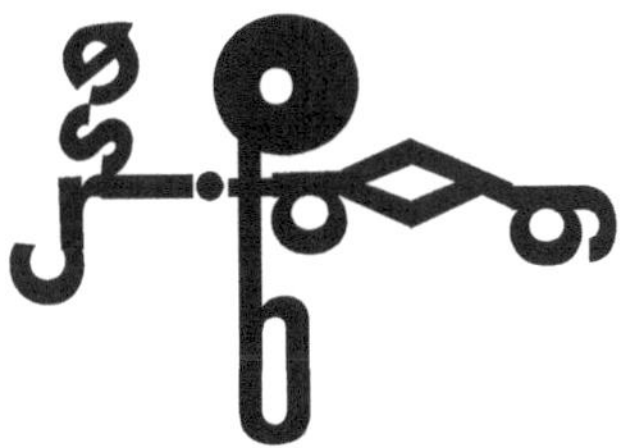

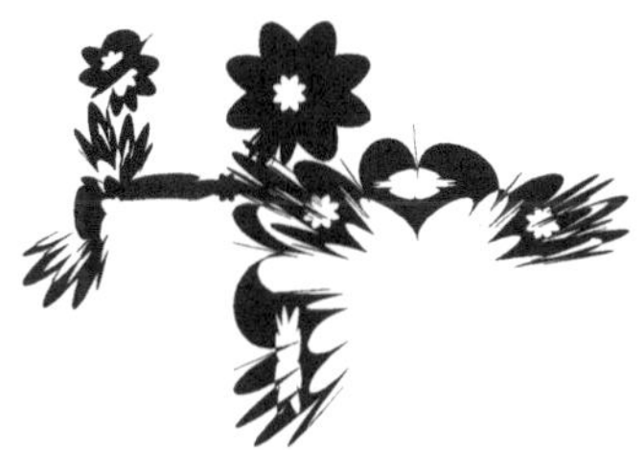

After some digital doodling in Photoshop I applied an effect to the letters just to see what would happen. This was the unexpected and delightful result.

In fact, I liked this piece so much, it became the basis for my business card! The design was finished in a digitally printed foil technique, rather than foil stamped, in silver and purple. The foil elements are eye catching, reflecting the light as the card is turned. While the reflective quality is very attractive and attention grabbing in person it makes it very difficult to photograph.

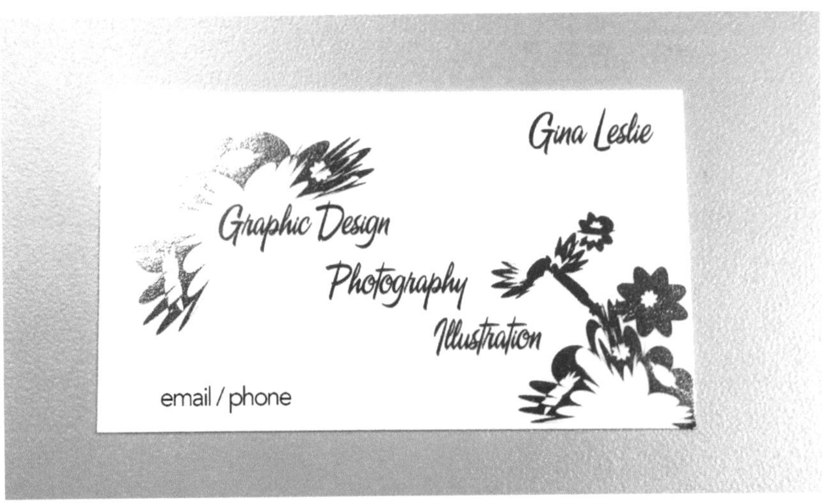

Travel To Ireland was initially created in 2014 and has been revised many times since. I have always wanted to go to Ireland. I even have a place to stay when I go. I just don't have the money to get there and pay for food, travel, etc. I had planned to go in late 2001, having received a modest amount of money from an unexpected inheritance and had been at my job long enough that I was eligible to take some vacation time. Then 9/11 happened and that plan went right out the window. Shortly after the tragic events, I was expected to fly to London for a work related convention. I wasn't afraid to fly, but I had concerns about getting stranded in another country and not being able to get back home if there were another attack and how I might pay for extended living accommodations abroad. I voiced these concerns to my boss, along with two other women in the office who said their husbands said they couldn't go. Their excuses for not going were perfectly acceptable to the boss. He fired me. I was out of work for 2 years and had to live on that inheritance money. I never did recover financially from that situation, but I still dream of going to Ireland some day*.

In it's present art form, the Trip To Ireland design looks like a woven textile. The maker in me is itching to try creating this as an actual woven piece.

*As of the publishing date of this book I have, at long last, booked my plane tickets to Ireland and am in the process of making travel plans with my host there. Sigils work!

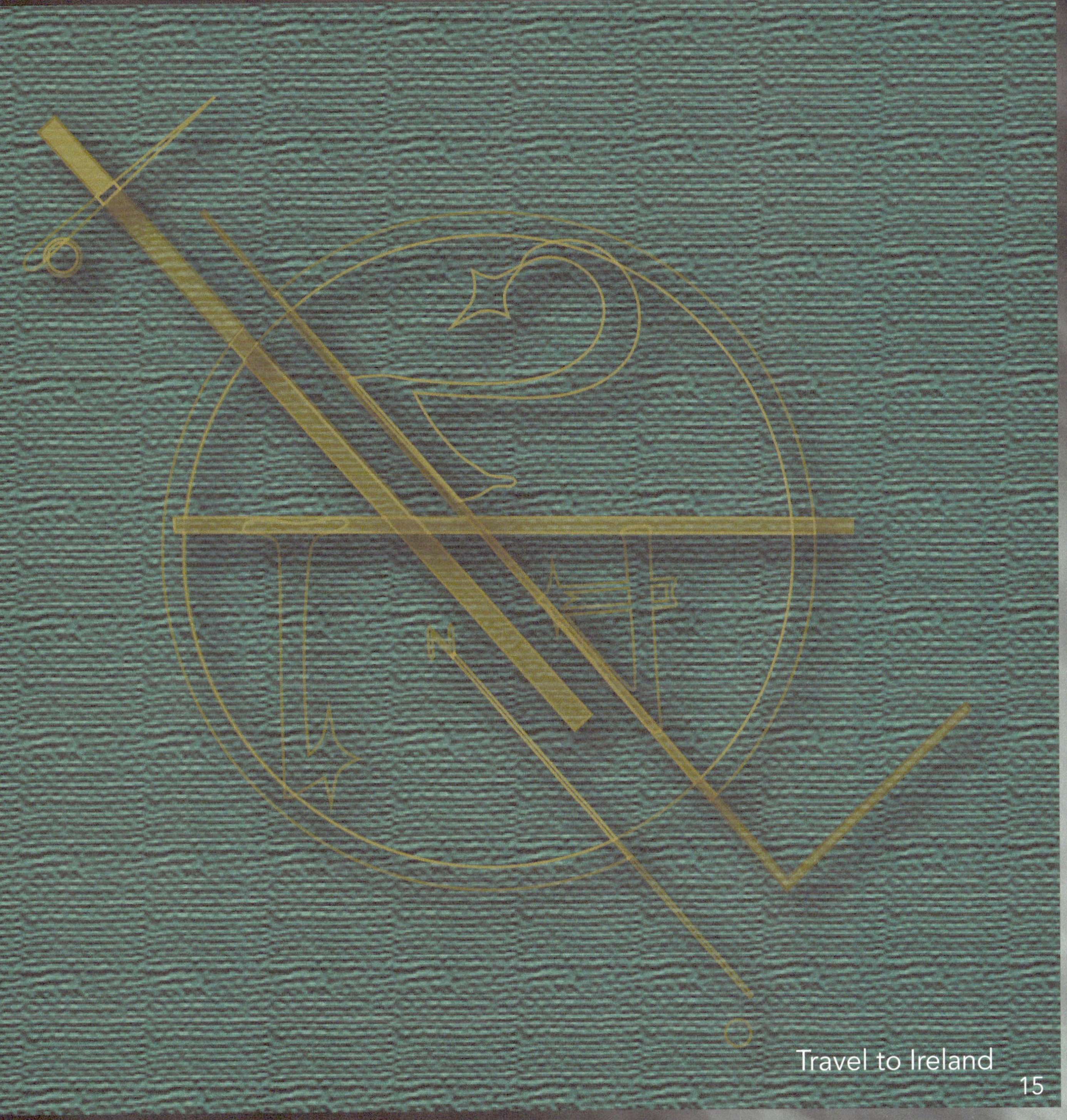
N

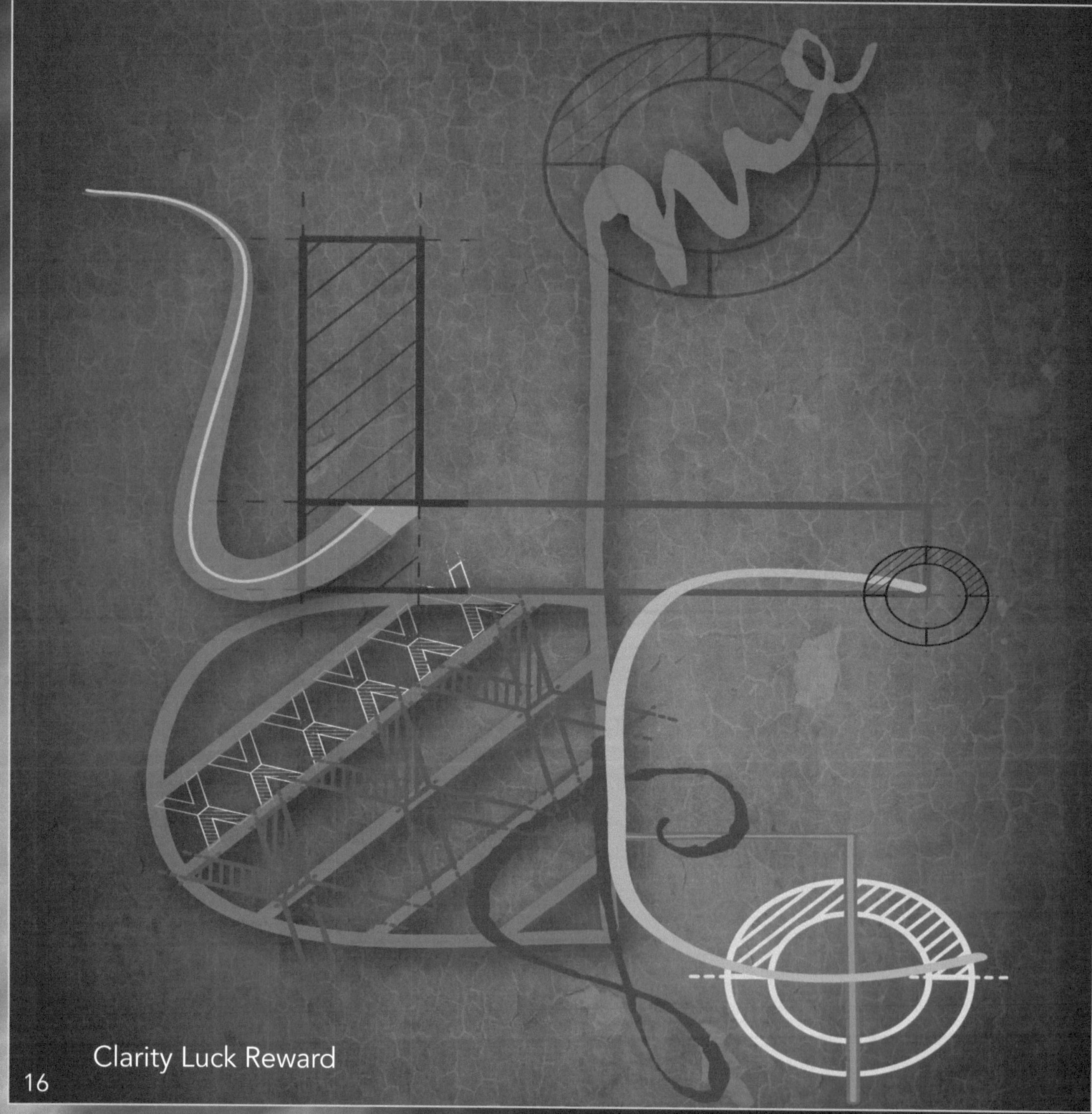

Clarity Luck Reward

The initial concept for this piece was to help me acquire an arts job I applied for. There was a time element involved and I'm obsessed with keys in that, for me, they remind me that I hold the keys to my future. I was obsessively reading, or quite likely re-reading the final Harry Potter book around time I made this sigil, so I think the snake and overall locket style was influenced by the Slytherin locket they were searching for in the book.

I had this artwork printed on an 8x8 canvas. My plan is to create a 3D assemblage — another of my "someday" projects.

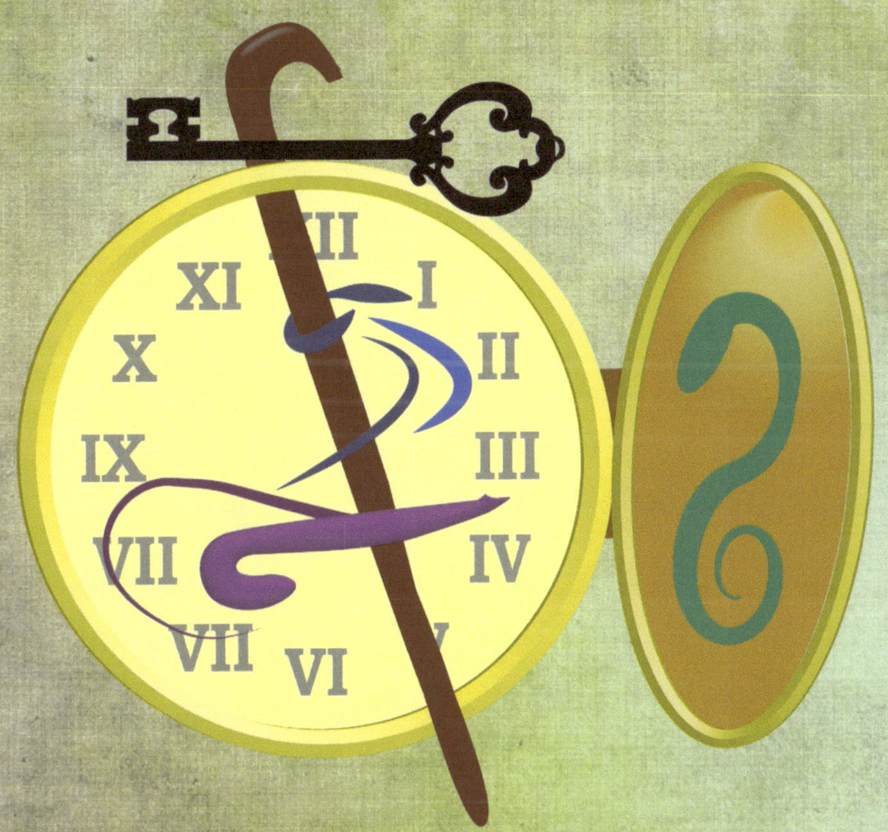

Behind the Scenes

A look inside the process

Recover Lost or Stolen Items - This one went through at least two designs on paper before I was satisfied with the results. You can see that I don't always stick with my original designs.

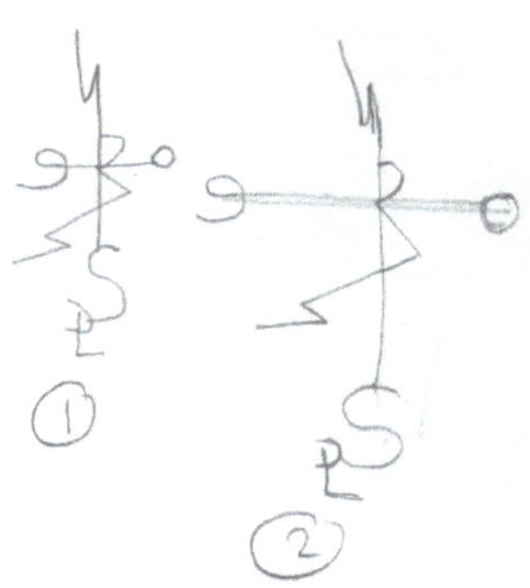

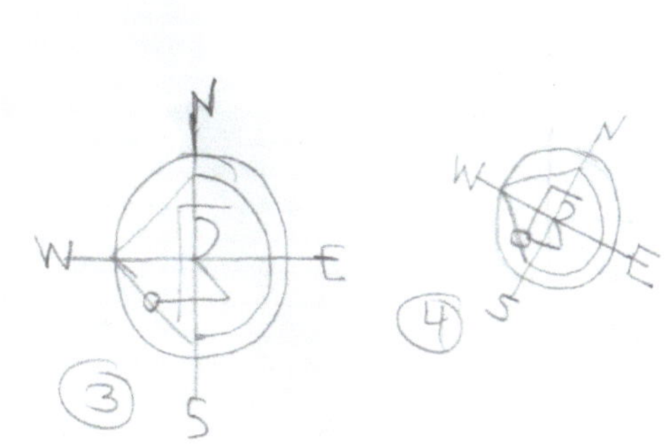

This was the first digital design based on the sketch.

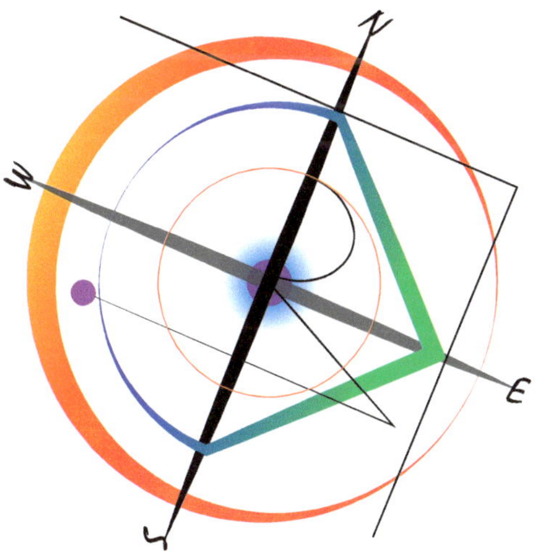

Having forgotten I had already done a digital version, I made another one when I started putting the book together.

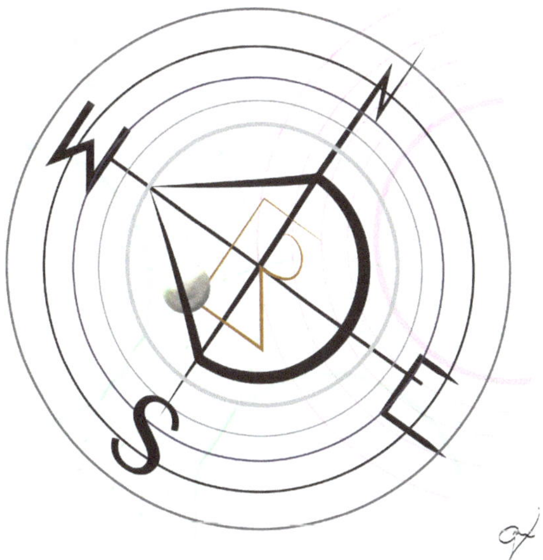

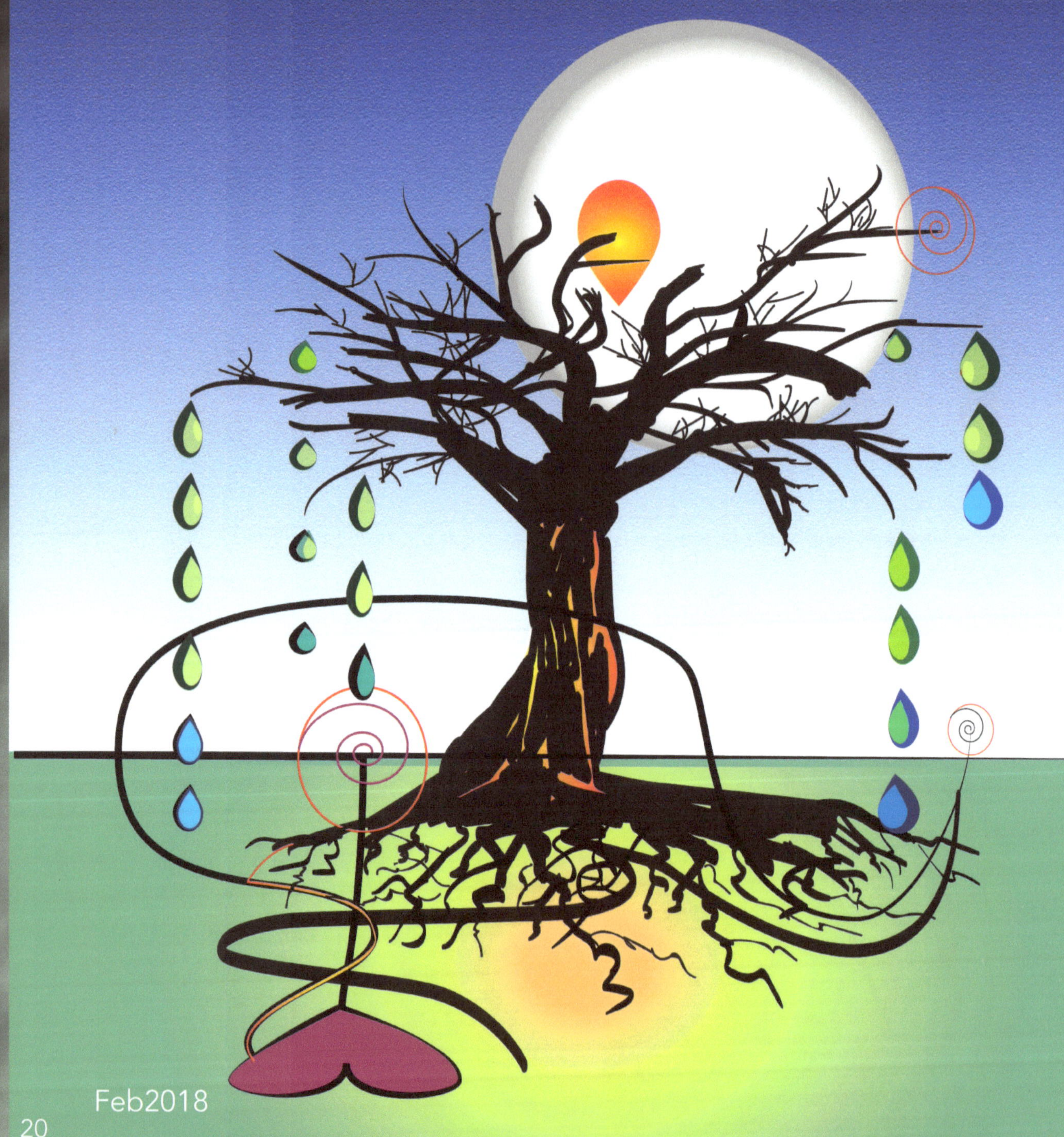
Feb2018

I did a magickal working with the pencil sketch of this sigil (which means I burned the original). It did not accomplish what I had hoped for, but it did plant quite a specific image in my mind. Below you can see my original pencil sketch which I photographed and opened in Illustrator, using it as a template to recreate and refine the design. The resulting digital design differs only slightly and started me thinking, initially, about a fountain which then led to thinking about a tree with drops of water coming off the leaves and dripping into a river.

The final artwork (on the preceding page) turned out quite close to what I had in mind. Since I burned the original sketch I didn't retain the words I used to create the sigil, and I don't remember the specific meaning, hence the date as a title. It doesn't really matter. I sent the message out to the universe. Sometimes sigils work, sometimes they don't, and sometimes they work in completely unexpected ways.

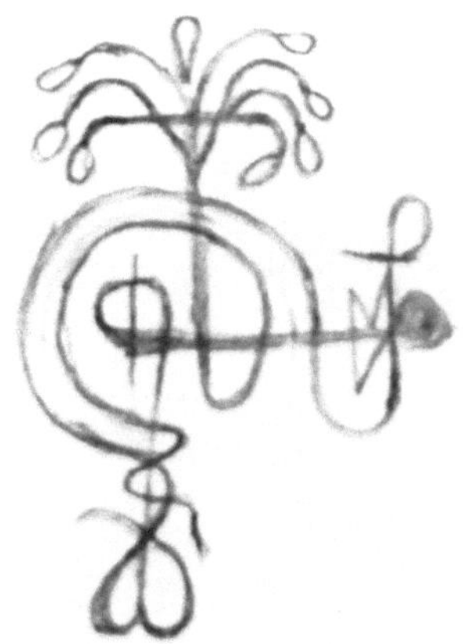

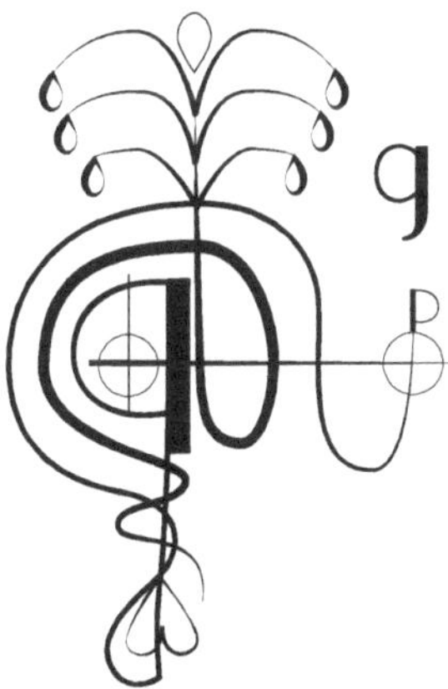

Sigil as Jewelry

In 2014 I played with the idea of making sigils designs to sell commercially. The sketches below (center and right) were based on the words Love, Health, & Happiness. As you see, I tried out many different configurations, none of which I really liked.

I made sigils as New Year's gifts for some friends. I went back to the commercial designs and came up with the design you see, circled on the left, to gift to a particular friend. In 2017 I was inspired to create a piece of jewelry from that sigil. This friend is a fan of Steampunk and owns a wonderful hat that has new and interesting elements added every time I see it. I thought this piece would make a fun and meaningful addition. Seems she thinks so too.

Be open to the inspiration!

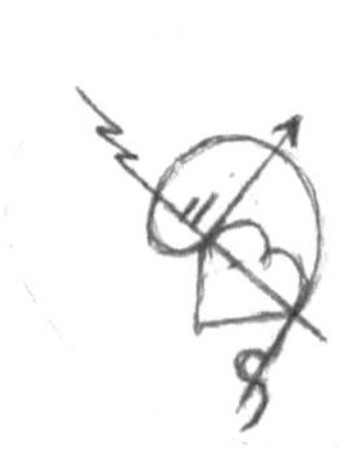

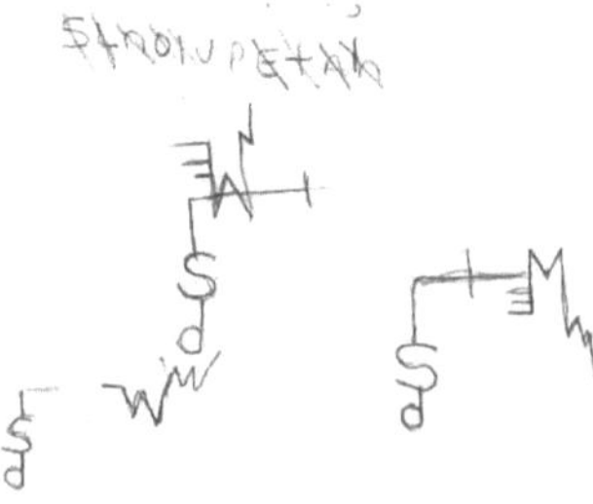

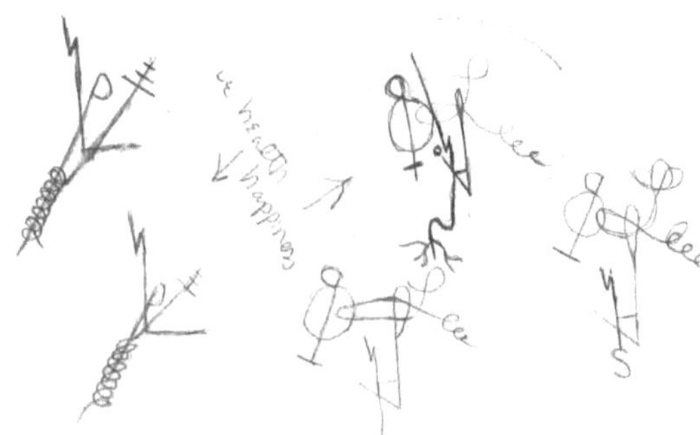

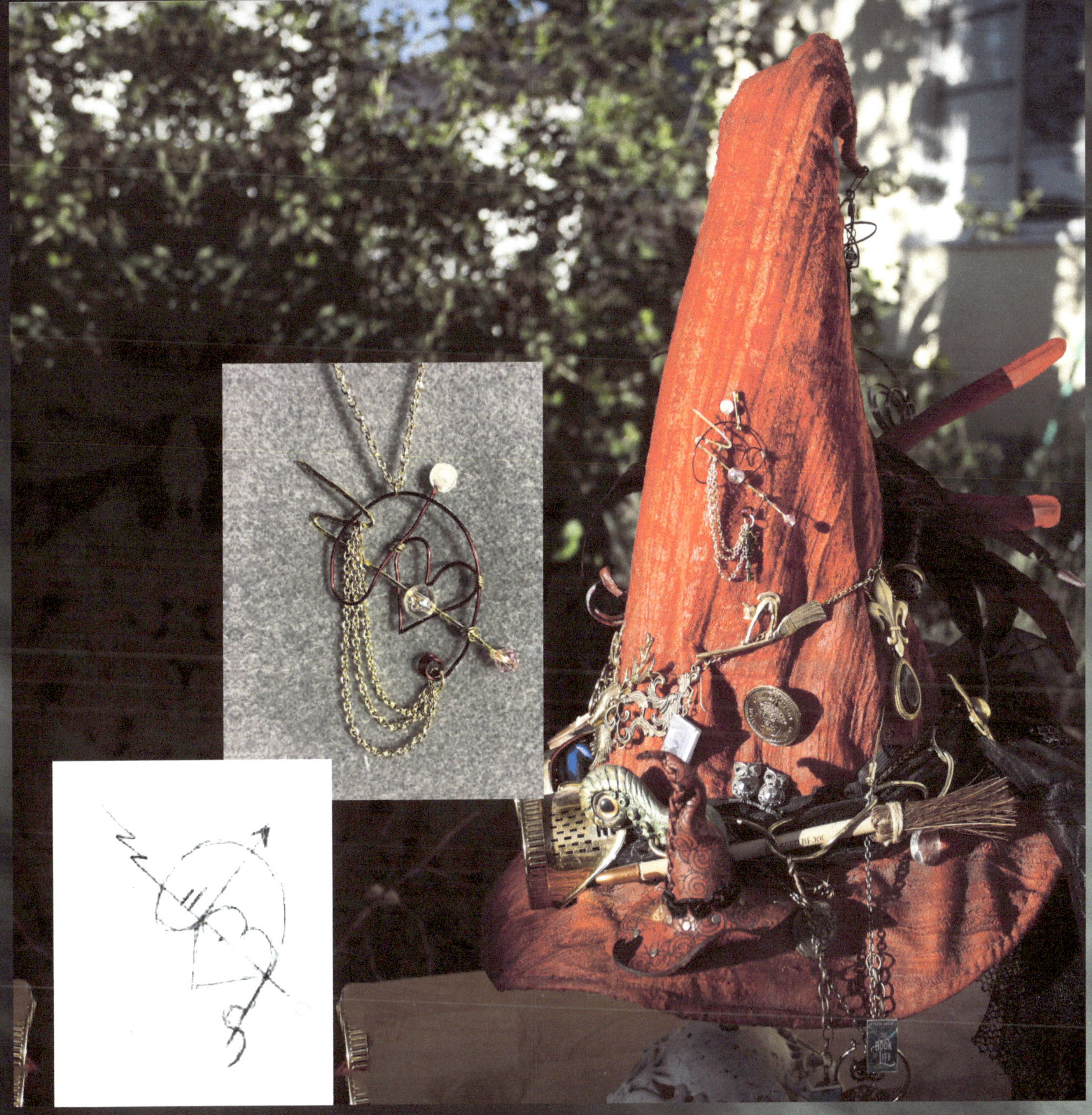

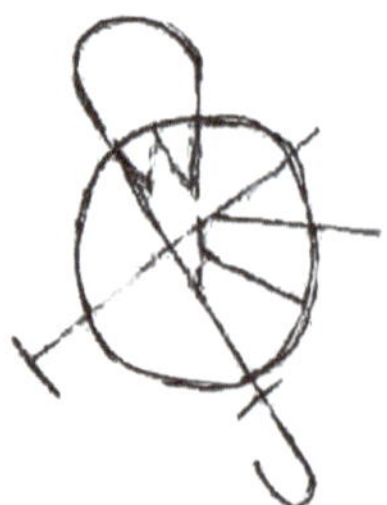

pencil drawing 1

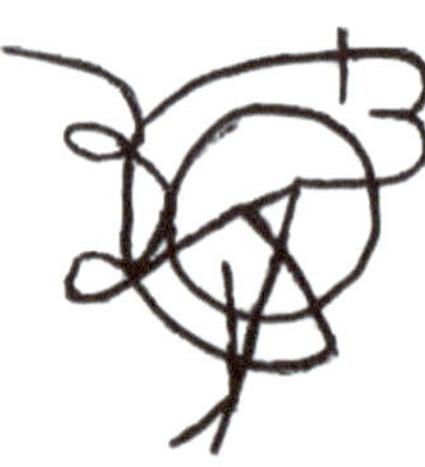

pencil drawing 2

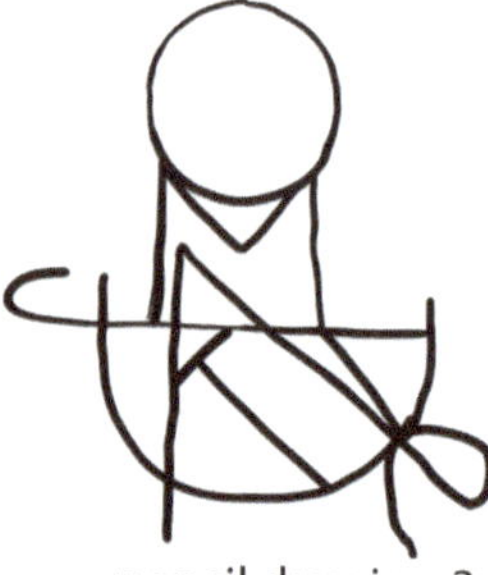

pencil drawing 3

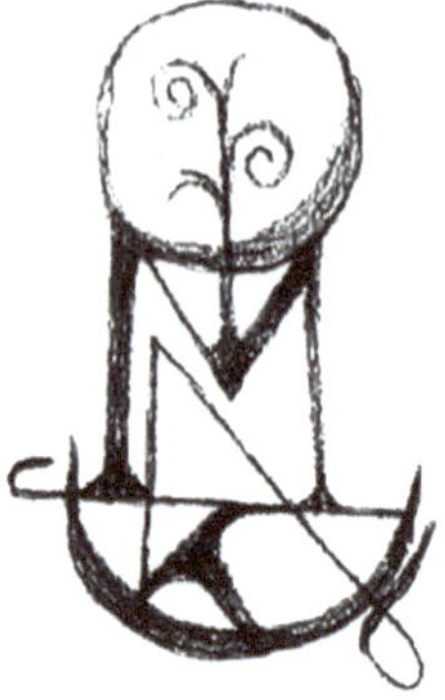

refined pencil drawing 3

I went through three idea sketches before I ended up with a combination I liked (drawing 3). I took that one and refined it some more. Then I digitized the drawing and when I was satisfied with the shapes I added color

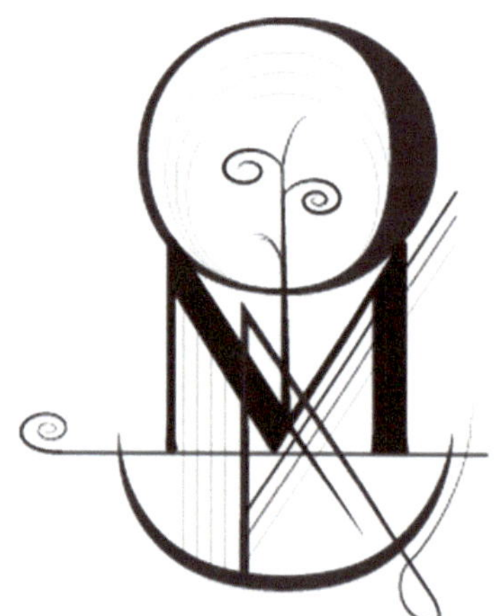

digitized pencil drawing

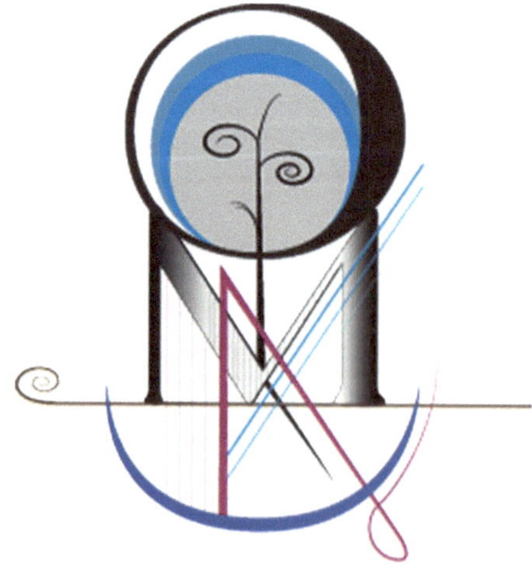

color final (?)
not sure any of them are ever final.

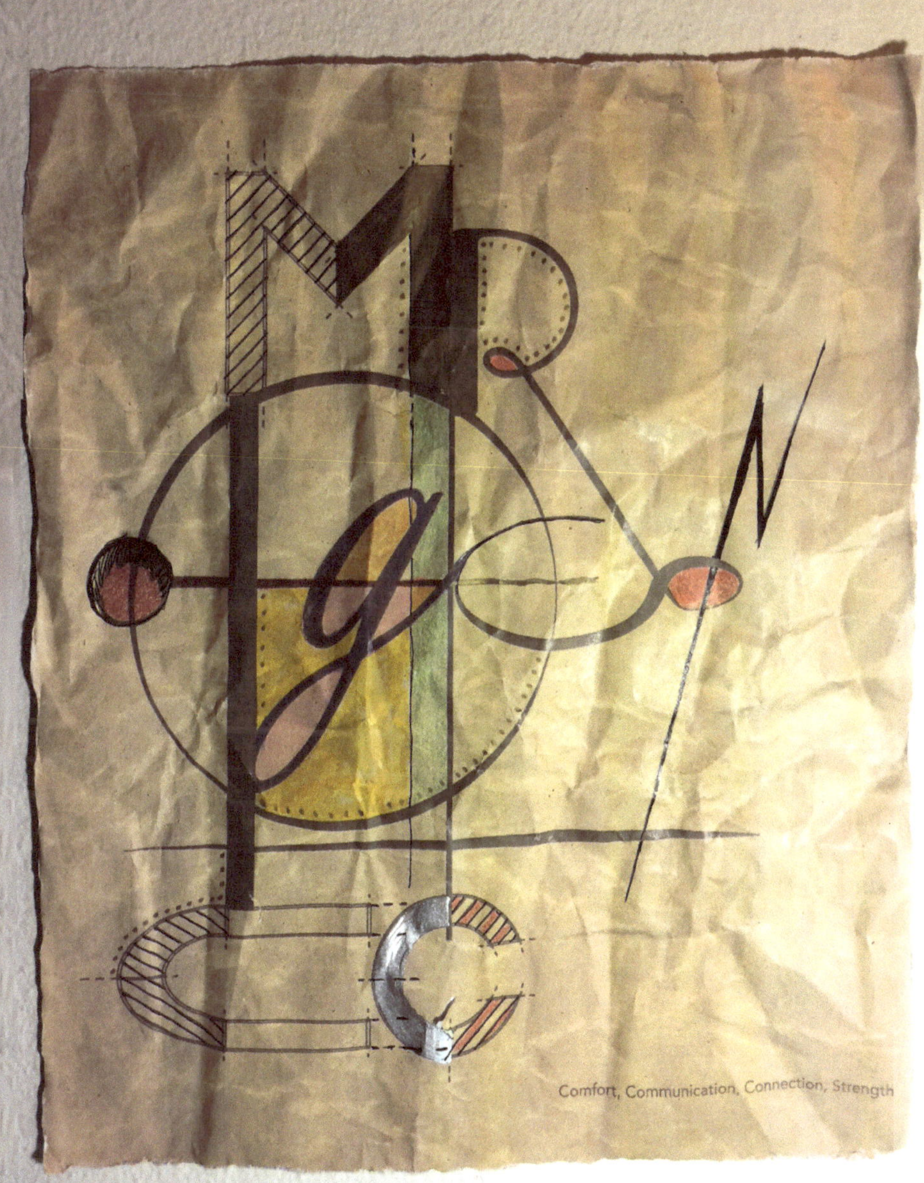

I made this one for someone who was grieving. The purpose of the sigil was not to take away their grief, but to give the person comfort, communication, connection and strength to help them get through their grief.

The crumpled paper represents how life can sometimes crumple us up, but we carry on anyway.

Comfort Communication Connection Strength

Sigil Inspiration Challenge #1

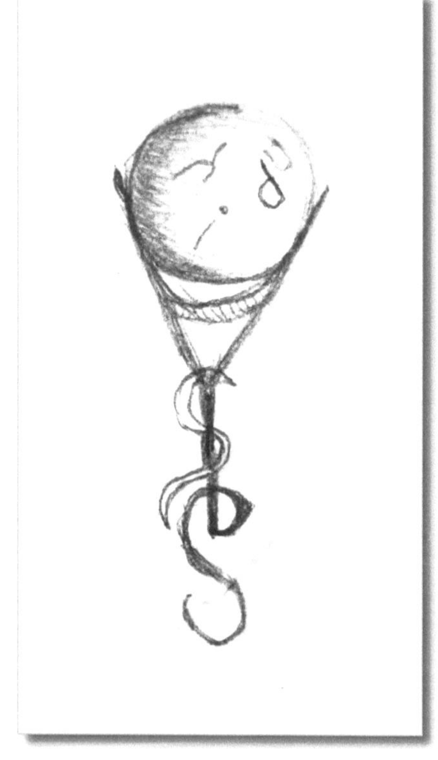

The intention for this sigil was
Travel Opportunity Prosperity Adventure.
It would be great if I could make money in some way while traveling around the country or around the world. I love photography so maybe I can get a gig as a travel photographer. Or I could teach a series of workshops on a cruise ship on how to compose more creative photos. There are probably other things I haven't even thought of. I'll keep my eyes open for the opportunity.

As I thought about turning this sigil into artwork I envisioned an orb in a tree branch with a ribbon tied to it. Then I focused on the snaky looking shape in the "y" of the branch and that got me thinking of a snake wrapped around someone's wrist and a hand coming up out of the water holding an orb (think the Lady of the Lake holding out Excalibur to the young King Arthur). The photo on the next page is my Sigil as Art interpretation.

The two pieces that follow are what my friends came up with in response to my challenge to create something based on this sigil. One is a musical composition created by Alfred Surenyan and the other is a motion graphic piece, created by Mandy Gough. I am honored to include their work in my book.

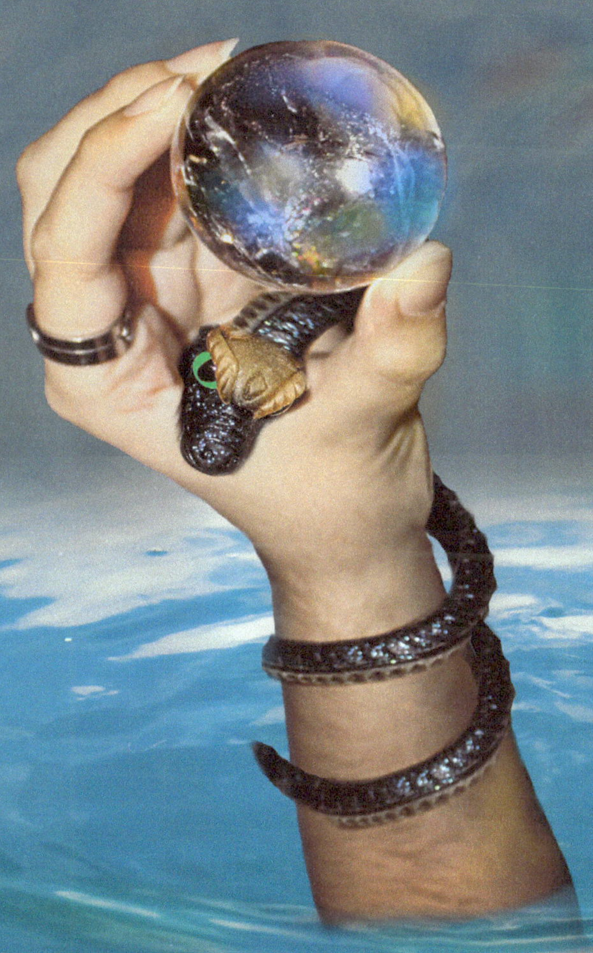

My concept with this wasn't to literally represent the sigil on the preceding page, but to illustrate the idea that starting with sigils can inspire other creative ideas.

My niece , Ana, was the hand model for this. When she saw the finished piece she said "it's like the person is drowning and saying 'quick, take this!'

I thought it was an interesting perspective, since it was so different than the meaning I saw in it. It inspired a completely different story for her.

Manifestation

Alfred composed a beautiful piece of music.
You can listen to it at https://www.youtube.com/watch?v=do9hy29rlLw

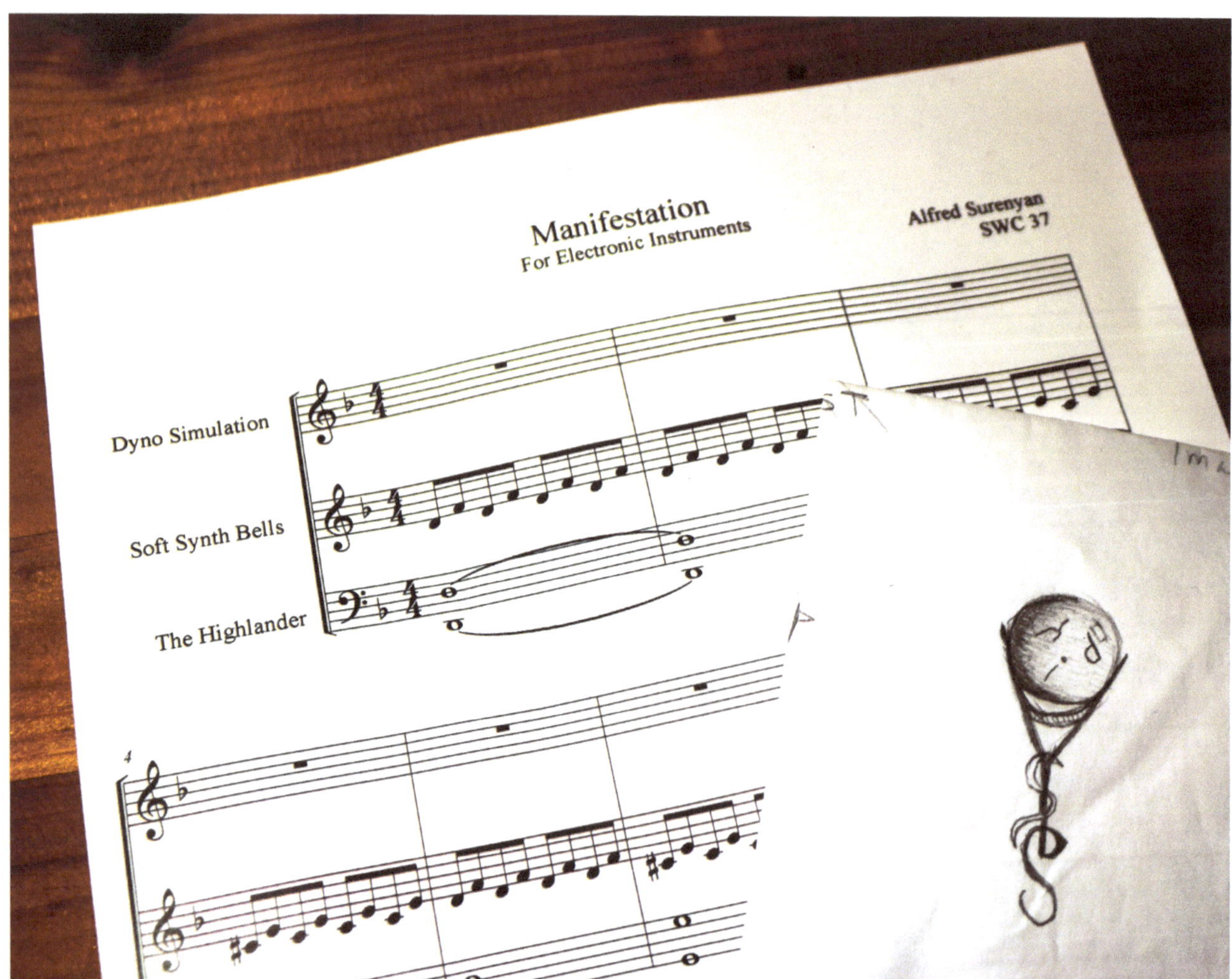

"Sigils are symbols and seals created for manifestation. I was inspired mostly from the circular shape on the top. I felt a mystery there as I did not know what the sigil represents. In order to create a circular unknown I used a minor key. The first theme is eerie and mysterious since, at first, it is unknown. The second theme is in a major key expressing an explosion of manifestation which comes from the sigil. As in any musical form, the first theme returns for a second statement, however orchestration is different for variation. Wind chimes are orchestrated between each section and at the end to create an overall magical feeling to the entire piece."

The music was composed using MIDI Orchestration with Digital synthesizer plug in with Logic Pro X.

Dr. Alfred Surenyan - Composer, Musicologist and Professor.
www.PashaMusic.com

Plotting Course

Mandy Gough created an amazing motion graphic.
You can watch it at https://youtu.be/EGpYyMBH8Hk

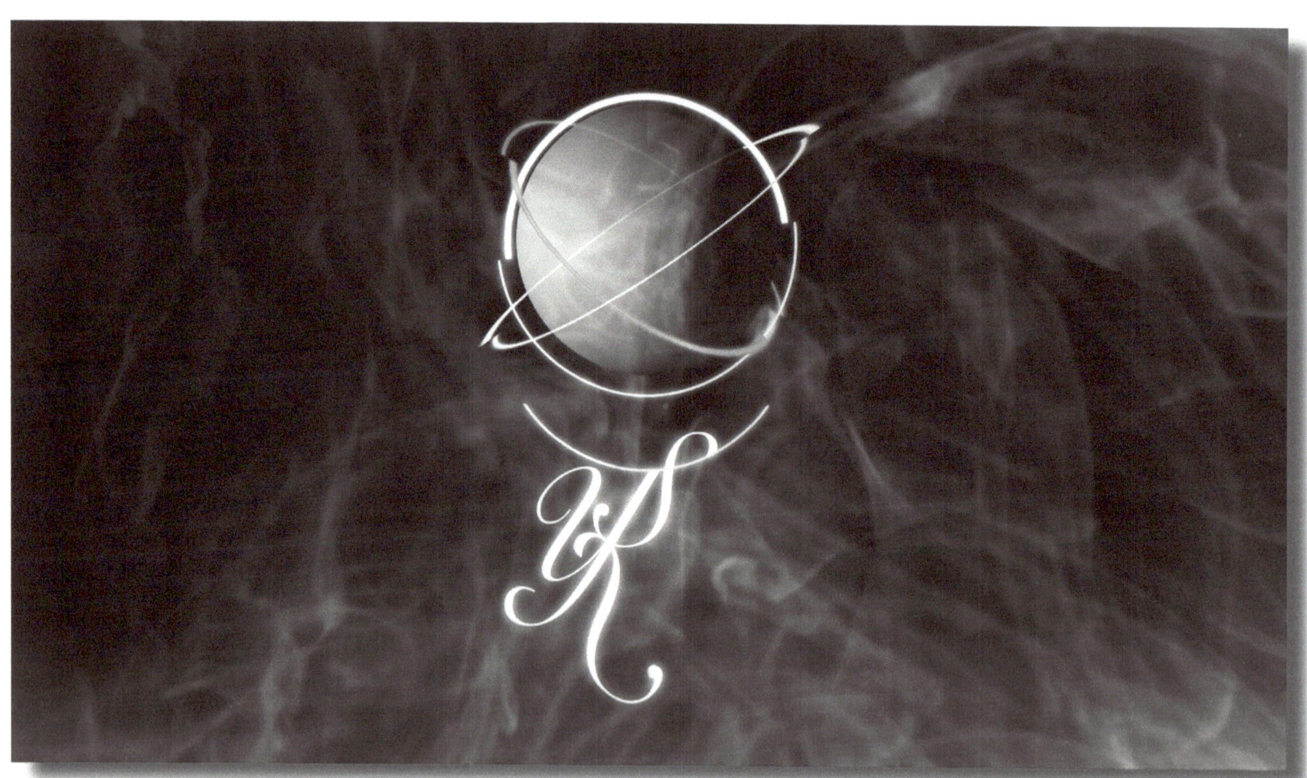

"When my good friend Gina shared that she was writing The Art of Sigils, and asked if I would be interested in creating an animation inspired by it, I was curious and excited to be involved. Working frequently with clients regarding a new product or service, my first task was to look further into sigils, and how to communicate the subject to the audience. I had some familiarity with the topic from our friendship already, so I was free to take it from there quickly, allowing a combination of technique and instinct to lead me. Starting with the "proudest" component, the sphere, or globe as I felt it, called out to take center stage. After anchoring it, the details fell into place like accessories to a fine lady's wardrobe, each element a pretty dripping bauble or supporting garnish I dressed her in, from stylized letters to smoky shroud. I had the added benefit of working with a selection from composer Alfred Surenyan's mystical score, also inspired by the sigil. A definite mood was conveyed and evolved into the mesmerizing, absorptive audio visual loop it became."

Mandy Gough - Creative & Art Director of Motion www.mandygough.com

(Mandy is also an amazingly creative herbalist. Check out her products at www.XoM3.com)

Sigil Inspiration Contest

Being pleased with the response I got from my friends with the first sigil challenge, I decided to try the same with a wider audience. I posted this sigil as a challenge on social media for anyone who wanted to enter using this design as their inspiration. As per the contest rules, all of the entries were posted to my Facebook page, but the three winning entries are included in this book.

All of the submissions were amazing! This sigil has inspired everything from a paper on space travel to a cookie recipe. The three entries I chose to include in the book are excellent examples of creativity that is not necessarily "Art". You can see all of the contest entries on my Facebook page @GinaLeslieAuthor.

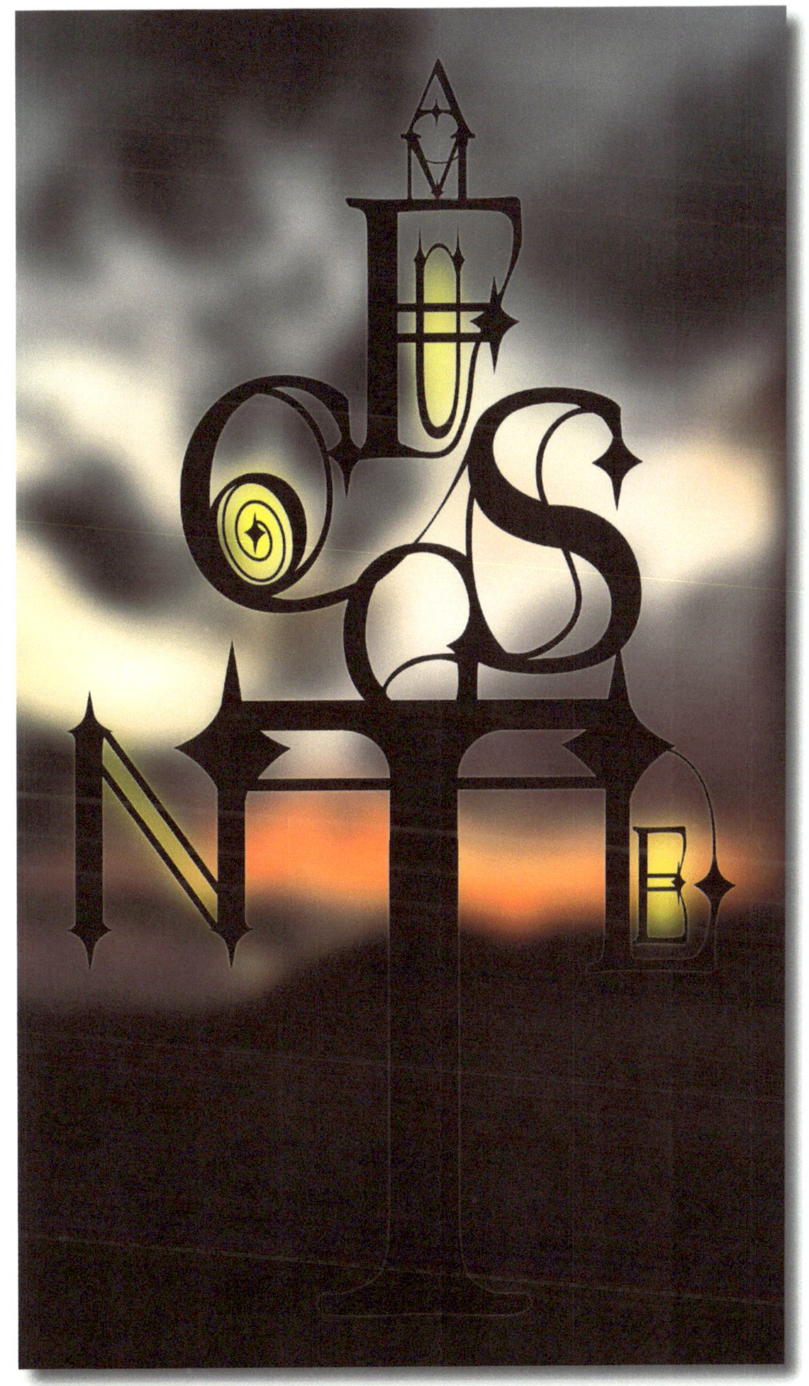

Fiery Boundaries

"I was inspired by this sigil as I immediately saw the word "nettles" in the graphic. First I saw the "n" and "s" and when I looked further into the sigil I saw the other letters all in different directions; upside down, right side up and sideways. I'm a wild food forager and recipe designer who is working on a recipe book using wild foods and this sigil spoke to me. It gave me this old time feel like early European with a lamp post and it made me think of snow and the holidays. I wanted to create a baked good that reminded me of the holidays and incorporate wild food (nettles in this case) to the recipe. I went foraging and found some random oranges on a tree in the middle of nowhere and added this to the mix.

My cookies are called "fiery boundaries". Nettles have little thorns on the stalks and leaves that disappear once cooked or dried. The plant teaches us boundaries and is full of nutrients and is earthy and salty in taste. The crystallized ginger is spicy and sweet and creates a fire inside us during the cold months. The orange rounds out the cookies by giving it the raw sweetness and bitterness from the zest."

Amanda Jones, Wild Food Forager and Recipe Designer
www.botanicalbusters.com / @foragingthebliss (instagram)
http://meetu.ps/c/2GHkP/pzsmP/d (Meetup)

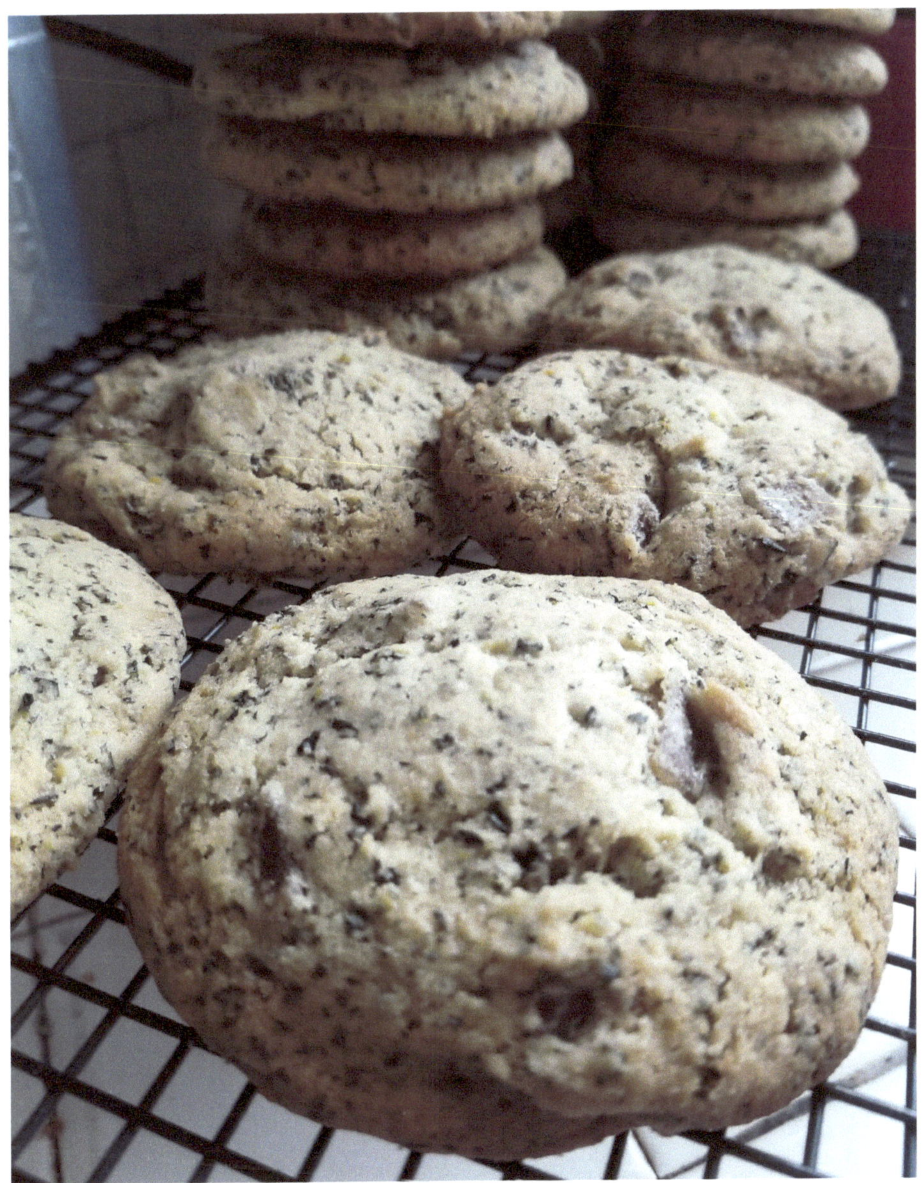

Textile Design

"Being a textile designer, I basically see pattern in everything around me. Talking of sigils I can totally see multiple shapes in them and I can even imagine how they would look as a repeat or a pattern!

I decided to create a few patterns based on the sigil posted on Facebook. I drew the motifs first by using ink and then scanned and manipulated them on computer to create the textile pattern."

Melody Hesaraky, Textile Designer

www.melodyhesaraky.com

This...

becomes this...

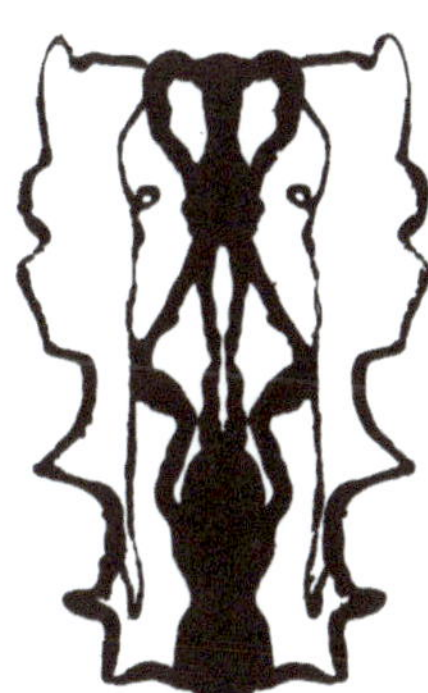

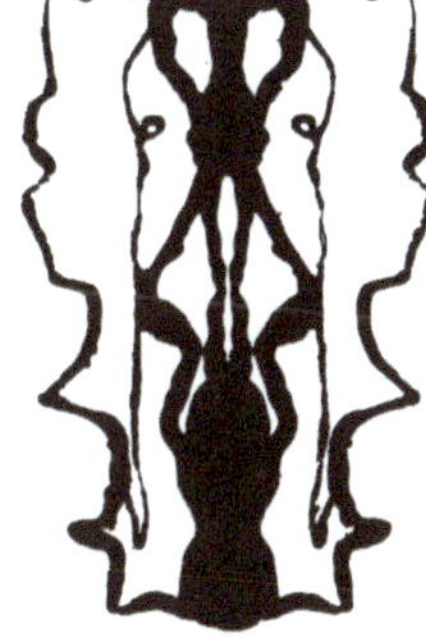

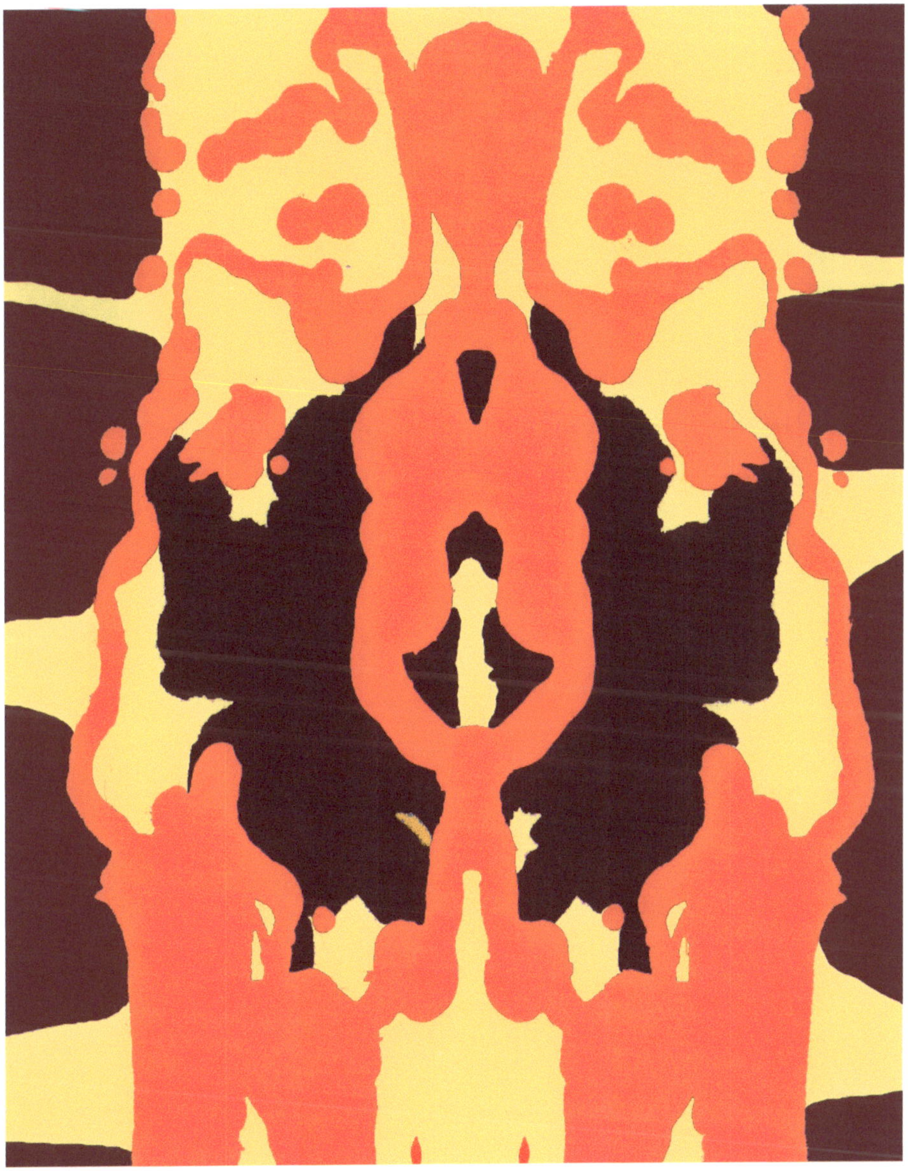

And this...

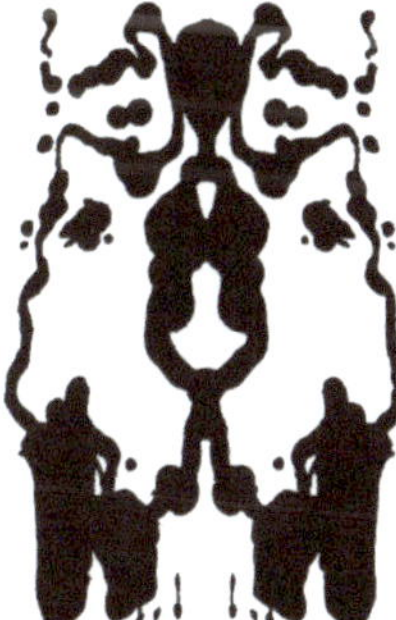

Quilled Snowflake

"This is a snowflake ornament made by a centuries old craft form called Quilling, also known as paper filigree. Although I have seen this art form before I have never tried it myself until now.

I was inspired by the four points of sigil and connected with how it imitated the graceful curls of Quilling."

Lisa Vig, Singer/Songwriter/Musician/Jill of Many Trades

www.hardlysisters.com

https://www.facebook.com/Hardly-Sisters-1426569164238366/?ref=br_rs

https://www.facebook.com/TraxxBand/

www.SoulPurposeBandLosAngeles.com

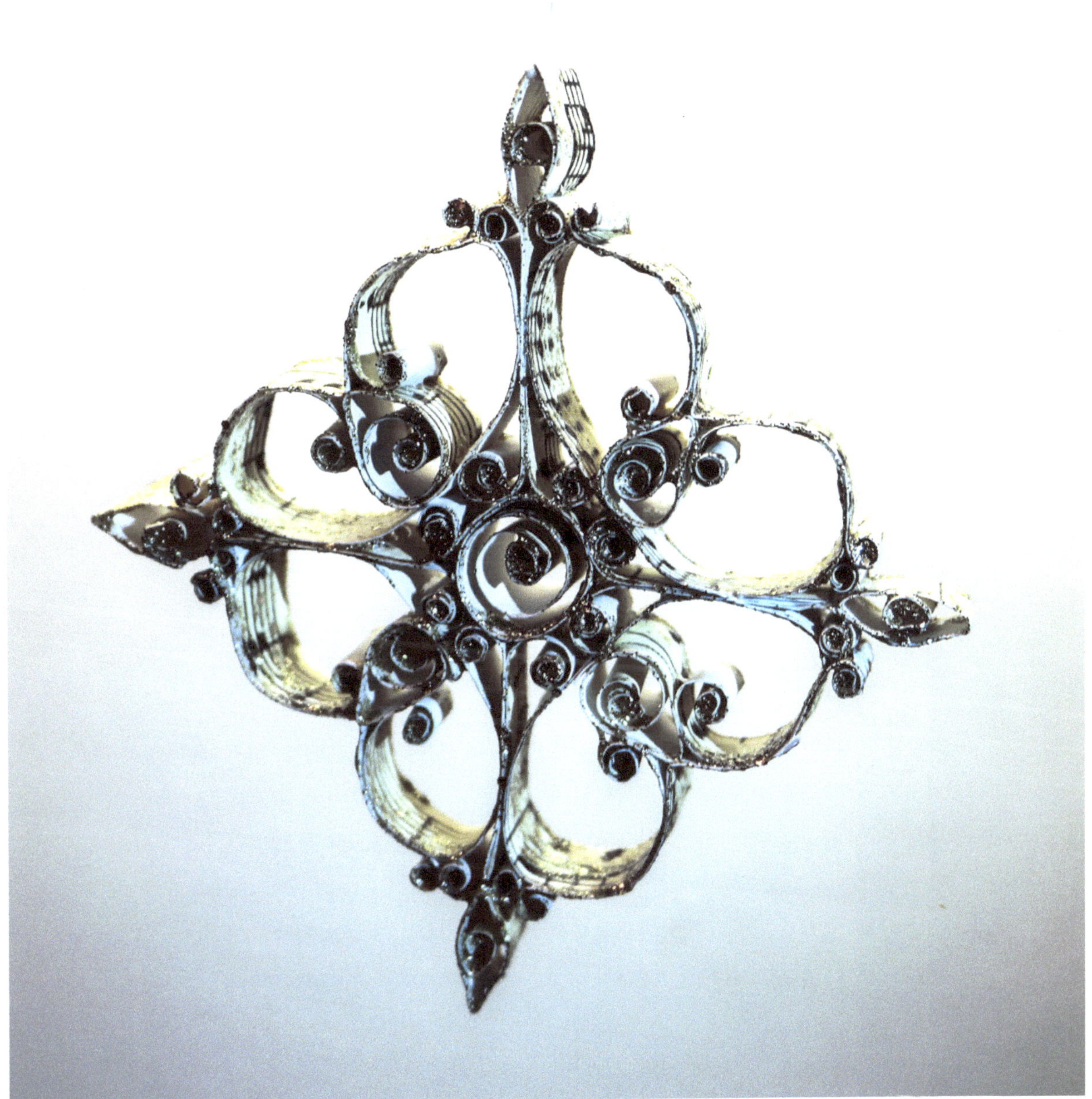

How to Make a Sigil

When I first published this book in 2018, my purpose was more to insprie creativity than specificlly teach how to make sigils, which I do in my classes. I did describe the sigil making process along the way, but from the reviews I read it's clear that I didn't get the point across. So I added this chapter to detail, step-by-step, how to make a sigil, how to charge; use it for manifesing a desired outcome. There are many ways to make sigils and lots of books that go into very minute detail. This is how I learned to do it. You may find a way that works better for you.

What Do You Want?

What are you manifesintg for? That's a tricky question because when I ask people that the most common answer I get is "money". Unless you're a coin collector, what you want is not money itself but something money can buy. And while you CAN manifest for World Peace, I suggest, to begin with, that you manifest for something more tangible so that you can see the results. Getting results gives your more confidence and more power behind future manifestations.

Try to distill the substance of your desire into 3 to 4 words. I have used whole sentences but since we'll be discarding letters along the way it makes more sense to make it short and sweet. You will charge or activate your sigil with your full intention later. As I mentioned elsewhere in this book, I went to Ireland for the first time in 2018. I had made a sigil in 2014 to manifest that trip. I have another unexpected opportunity to go back to Ireland in 2021, but COVID-19 is playing havoc with those plans. So as an example for you, I'm manifesting for "Successful Ireland Trip 2021".

1. Write your intention — **successful Ireland trip 2021**

2. Cross out repeating letters — **successful Ireland trip 2021**

3. Rewrite the remaining letters. I mix up the order so I'm not looking at actual words. — **successful Ireland trip 2021**

1 s o u 2 c p e t f d l n i r a

When I make sigils for other people, I give them the numerical value of the letters I'm using just in case they work with numbers. There are 16 letters in this sigil. I don't do this if I'm making a sigil for myself because I don't work with numerology.

Start arranging the letters one by one. You can start with whichever letter you want. In general, I start with the letter O (there's almost always an O).

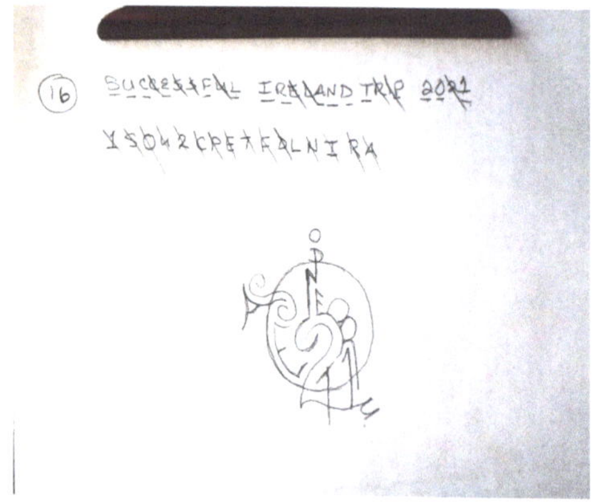

4. Arrange the letters any way that feels right to you.

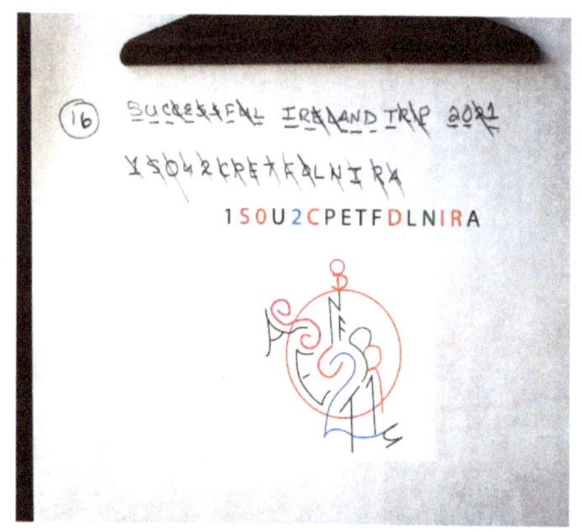

4a. I made it in colors so you can see how I used the letters.

Sometimes if the letters have the same basic shape (like W and M), I will only use it once or combine two similar shapes (like V and A). In this example, I used the number 1 and the letter L in the same shape. Sometimes I repeat letters. The letters don't have to remain looking like letters. If something tells you to make the F into a bird's head go with it. If you work with runes, astrology and/or numerology and it feels like you should add some of that to your design do it. Let your intuition guide you.

I work very intuitivly. If I get a feeling I should start with the letter X instead of O, I do that. If I need to repeat, echo, or combine letters or shapes I do that. Aplogies to the more structural minded people out there.

Keep working until you feel that it's done. You can see that I made a second design layout. I like the first one better. If you don't like what you've come up with, start over. I usually "feel" when it's done. I've had some that just never felt right. That tells me either what I'm manifesting isn't for me, or it isn't for me at this time. Any time I have stubbornly tried to force a sigil, I just end up angry and frustrated (not good mindsets for magickal working).

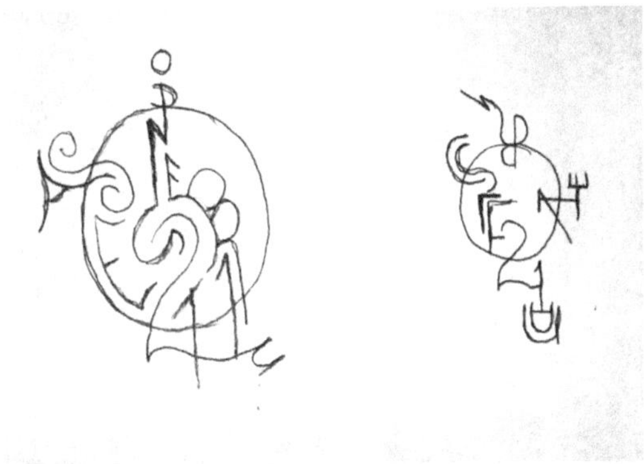

5. Start over as many times as you need to.

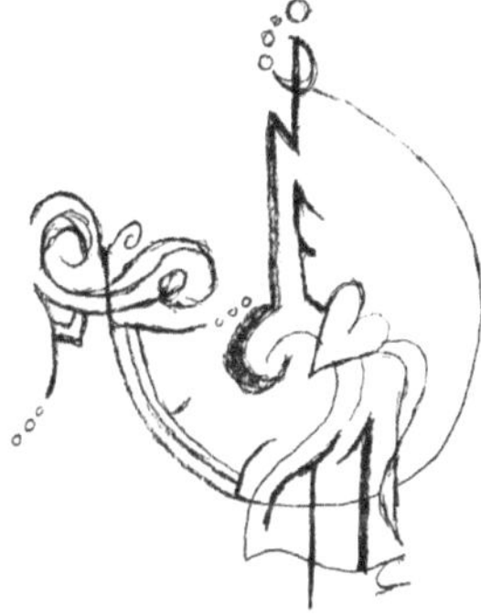

6. Embelish the design if you want.

When you're making a sigil intended for a magickal working (rather than creative inspiration), it doesn't have to be "pretty". It doesn't have to "look like" something. I've done some sigils that were very basic sketches in a very short period of time. They were just as effective as the "pretty" ones that I make.

Let's Talk Ethics

As a general rule manifesting something that will take away someone's free will is unethical. I recommend you don't do it.

Someone came to me recently and asked if I could curse their boss (hey, we've all been there). If you read the Harry Potter books you remember when Bellatrix tells Harry "you have to mean it" when he was trying to curse her after she killed Sirius. It's true. You have to mean it. I do know how to curse, but I have never encountered anyone who was worth the amount of time and effort it takes to curse someone. Also, that's not the kind of energy I want to add to the world.

Instead of cursing the boss, I had them bind the bad behavior that was making them so miserable at work (protection/binding spell). Them I had them envision what a happier, healthier work environment would look like and manifest that.

By not doing the curse, I helped the person proctect themself; manifest a better work environment; and not have guilt about cursing someone because I know for a fact that they would have been devestated if some terrible thing happend to their boss after they cursed them.

Everything has a cost. Magick is no different. Make sure you are willing to "pay the coin" for what you want. Also, be careful what you wish for. Which bring us to...

Love Magick.

Love magick might be the most dangerous and unpredictable magick there is. Making someone love you is taking away their free will, and therefore, unethical. Don't get me wrong, it can be done. But why would you want someone who is only with you by force? And what if you find out that this person really isn't the soul mate you thought they were? Or what if they smother you with love and attenton (not in a good way)? Getthing them out of your life might be even more difficult than bringing them in.

I don't think any of us are wise enough to know who specifically is best for us. If you are determined to bring a love relationship into your life, focus on asking for opportunity and compatability–not manifesting for a specific person.

Charging and Releasing

When you are satisfied that your sigil is complete, you will charge and release it to The Universe or the diety of your choice if you work with those.

Hold your sigil in your hands and try to invision your desire. If you are manifesting to find an object, imagine holding it or using it. If you are manifesting for a trip, envision being there. What does it look like? How does it feel, sound, smell, taste? Make it as real as you can in your mind and body. Don't be concerned about how it will manifest. Just envision it as if it is already real.

When you have a clear vision or feeling of it in your mind, physically blow all of that into the sigil you are holding. Blow that vision into the sigil three times. After you have done that, you can do several things next; you can put it away somewhere where you won't see it anymore (maybe in a book you don't open very often or an old journal); you can tear it up and bury it or burn it

Now let The Universe take over and make it happen. Be aware of 'coincidences'. Does a friend keep asking you to go to yard sales or swapmeeting and you've been declining? If you're manifesting for a physical, thing maybe you should take them up on their offer.

If you are manifesting for a trip, be on the look out for opportunities. Maybe there is a contest, and the prize is a trip to where you want to go. If you're manifesting for a better job and an opportunity comes along for a job that is not in your field but looks interesting, and something you can do explore that option. Sometimes we're so focused on getting "The Thing" we want the way we think it's supposed to be that we miss opportunities that are right in front of us.

I was at a job for years where I was miserable because my boss was an ass. I applied for job after job to go somewhere else with no success. I manifested for a new, better job. I manifested a binding that he couldn't do anything to hurt me anymore (that one worked!). I finally manifested that HE would get the job offer of his dreams; thereby leaving and not being my manager any more. Apparently the job of his dreams was not having me as an employee to deal with because shortly thereafter a manager in a different part of the company asked if I could come work for him. I relocated to an office a mile away from "Bad Manager" and had the best working relationship I've ever had with a boss while doing basically the same work for the same company, just in a different locaton. So, I got my better job, just not the way I expected.

I hope I have given you enough information to manifest your desires through sigils. Happy crafting!

Step Through the Gateway

Most of my designs are 2D, but this process can be used to inspire any creative output - drawing, painting, sculpture, music, dance, baking, decorating, writing - anything that speaks to you. Allow yourself to be creative and follow your muse!

My advice is: if the execution of your idea is not flowing smoothly in the direction you planned on, don't try to force it into being what you think it should be. Let the shapes or thoughts that emerge inform the design. Very often in my design process, regardless of the medium I am using, I find that when I allow the process to flow rather than force it to be what I think I want, it typically turns out better than what I had planned in the first place. You don't have to be satisfied with your first thought. If that leads to someplace different, go there. Remember the tree branch with the orb that ended up becoming a hand rising out of the water with a snake? That's a perfect example of where following the direction of where the work leads to you can bring pleasant, if unexpected, results.

I would love to hear from you and see what you come up with in your own exploration of sigils and creativity. I encourage you to share your thoughts with me about this book. I can't wait to see your sigil–inspired creations and hear about your thought process behind them via email or on social media. Be sure to tag your posts #TheArtOfSigilsBook.

If you enjoyed The Art of Sigils, please leave a review on the site where you purchased the book or other sites that allow book reviews, including Amazon, Good Reads and my Facebook page.

Thanks and good luck with your creative exploration!

Services:

I teach in-person and virtual classes on making and using sigils.
I make sigils for people who don't want to make their own.
Readings to make you a magickal potion for what you need.

Email:	ginalauthor@gmail.com
Facebook:	@GinaLeslieAuthor
Instagram:	@TheArtOfSigils
Twitter:	@TheArtOfSigils
Website:	www.TheArtOfSigils.com
Newsletter signup:	http://bit.ly/2E2Fr1S
Sigil or potion appointment:	https://calendly.com/sigilsandmore/sigilcall

ABOUT THE AUTHOR

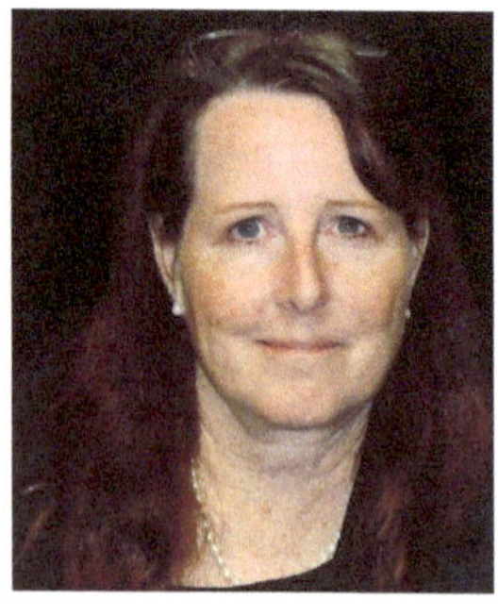

Growing up in Southern California, Gina Leslie began writing in her 'tweens as a much needed mode of private self-expression and catharsis. Out on her own after high school, her perseverance saw her through a series of dead-end jobs and part-time college attendance to earning her BA in Art from Cal State Northridge. Through the years she also picked up many other artistic habits and hobbies, including fine art photography, quilting, painting, sculpting, woodworking, lampworking, sewing, and more. Processes fascinate her, and she is eager to learn how things are done and what makes things tick.

Always knowing that there is more in the world than what we perceive with our five senses, Gina started on a path of metaphysical discovery in the early 2000s. She explored psychic development, herbalism, Shamanism, sigils and other forms of magick, religion and spiritualism. From 2008 through 2014 she was the president of the Los Angeles chapter of Pagan Pride, overseeing the global organization's largest annual Pagan Pride Day events and helping to move the festival from a secluded park to it's, very public, current home at Rainbow Lagoon Park in Long Beach. It was during this immersion in the pagan community and access to many skilled teachers that she discovered her talent for sigil making. Her natural inclination for creativity then lead her to develop her sigils into artwork.

Recently she decided to combine her sigil making, creativity and writing. The Art of Sigils is her first published book. She can often be found working behind the scenes of non-profit organizations providing graphic design services and planning events which bring people together, promote tolerance, support The Arts, and nurture creativity.

Other Books By Gina Leslie
(to be published)

The Magic In Your Stars

This easy to follow book has color photos and instructions for manifesting your desire through a paper folding process

Sleeping Beauty's Nightmare
(working title)

This tale of betrayal and madness was inspired by the old tale of The Sleeping Beauty and by Neil Gaiman's The Sleeper and the Spindle. It's definately NOT fairytale for children.

Sign up for Gina's newsletter at http://bit.ly/2E2Fr1S to receive monthy sigils, for inspiration or manifestation and to be notifed of the publication dates for future books.

www.ingramcontent.com/pod-product-compliance
Lightning Source LLC
LaVergne TN
LVHW070149110826
845147LV00002B/355

9781732204508